Kate Hefford

Gertru

Knowledge a

Gertrude

(The Cry)

And

Knowledge And A Girl

(The Snow White Case)

two plays by

Howard Barker

Calder Publications
London

First published in Great Britain in 2002
by Calder Publications Ltd,
51 The Cut, London SE1 8LF

ISBN 0 7145 4326 8

Applications for a license to perform these plays should be made to:
Judith Daish Associates, 2 St. Charles Place, London W10 6EG.

British Library Cataloguing in Publication Data
A catalogue of this title is available from the British Library

Library of Congress Cataloging in Publication Data
A catalogue of this title is available from the Library of Congress

Set in 9/10pt Times by Kolam Information Services Pvt. Ltd., India
Printed and bound by MPG Books Ltd, Bodmin, Cornwall

For Victoria Wicks

GERTRUDE

(*The Cry*)

For the Fraction

CHARACTERS

Gertrude	A Queen
Claudius	A Prince
Cascan	Servant to Gertrude
Hamlet	An Heir
Isola	Mother of Claudius
Ragusa	A Young Woman
Albert	A Duke of Mecklenburg

1

The orchard at Elsinore. A king asleep on the ground.

GERTRUDE:	(*Entering*) I should
	Surely
	I should
	Me
CLAUDIUS:	(*Entering*) No
GERTRUDE:	Me
	Let me
CLAUDIUS:	It must be me who
GERTRUDE:	Why not me
CLAUDIUS:	Me who
GERTRUDE:	HE IS MY HUSBAND WHY NOT ME
	(*Pause*)
CLAUDIUS:	Because he *is* your husband it must be me
GERTRUDE:	Let me kill
	Oh let me kill for you
	(*Pause*)
CLAUDIUS:	I'm killing
	Me
	(*Pause*)
GERTRUDE:	KILL MY HUSBAND THEN KILL HIM
	FOR ME
	(*A fractional pause*)
CLAUDIUS:	Strip
GERTRUDE:	Strip?
CLAUDIUS:	Naked
GERTRUDE:	Strip naked yes
CLAUDIUS:	Let me see the reason I am killing
GERTRUDE:	(*Tearing off her clothes*) Yes
	Yes
CLAUDIUS:	And if he stirs
	If his eyes open in his agony
	Show him the reason he is dying
	Let him see what I have stolen
	What was his
	And what now belongs to me

THE THING
THE THING
LET THE DYING DOG'S EYES SWIM
YOUR
(*Pause*)
He's not a dog
(*He shrugs*)
I called him a dog

GERTRUDE: Do it now
CLAUDIUS: If anyone's a dog
GERTRUDE: DO IT NOW
CLAUDIUS: It's me
            (*Gertrude positions herself above the head of the sleeping man, tilted, provocative*)
GERTRUDE: Poison him
            (*Claudius goes to kiss Gertrude. She shuts her eyes, averts her face*)
            Poison him
            (*Claudius takes the phial from his clothing. He kneels by the sleeping man. He pours the fluid into the man's ear. Gertrude seems to vomit in her ecstasy. Her cry mingles with the cry of the sleeping man who shudders*)
            Fuck me
            Oh fuck me
            (*Claudius and Gertrude couple above the dying man. All three utter, a music of extremes. A servant enters holding a garment, and attends*)

2

CASCAN: All ecstasy makes ecstasy go running to a further place that is its penalty we know this how well we know this still we would not abolish ecstasy would we we would not say this ever-receding quality in ecstasy makes it unpalatable on the contrary we run behind it limping staggering I saw it there I saw it there
            (*He laughs*)
            A haunting mirage on the rim of life
            (*He extends the gown for Gertrude*)
            Eventually I can't help thinking eventually it

lures us over a cliff so what why not a cliff is a
cliff worse than a bed a stinking bed inside a
stinking hospital no give me the cliff do put this
on the cliff every time your nakedness is so perfect hide it hide it keep it for the dark or these
rare acts
Madame
(*Gertrude goes to Cascan and is enclosed in the
gown*)
And what magnificence your cry a cry I am if I
may say so not only familiar with but something
of a connoisseur of its varieties this cry I heard
beyond the orchard wall and marvelled at its
depth its resonance I do not honestly expect to
hear its like again what could give birth to such a
cry a dying husband an impatient lover supre-
mely beautiful
(*Gertrude weeps*)
But unrepeatable surely
(*Her shoulders heave in her grief*)
Yes
Yes
We are surely near to the cliff now oh so close to
the cliff

GERTRUDE:	(*wailing*) MY HUSBAND
CASCAN:	Yes
GERTRUDE:	MY HUSBAND
	(*She lifts her hands helplessly*)
	OH HOW I LOVED MY HUSBAND
CASCAN:	Yes
	Yes
GERTRUDE:	Little boy

Oh little boy
(*Cascan and Claudius watch the suffering of
Gertrude. A pause*)
I called him little boy
(*She recovers*)
He was ten years older than
No
Twelve not ten
Twelve
Twelve years older than
If anyone was little it was me

LITTLE GIRL
That would have made more sense I think
(*She gathers up her garments*)
A sweet love silly possibly some loves are silly
others find them irritating can you see my shoe
simplicity offends the world and we were very
simple shoe blue shoe ALL MY SHOES ARE
BLUE NOW YOU INSIST ON IT
(*She smiles at Claudius through her tears. He
brings the missing shoe to her. Leaning on
Cascan with one arm, she lifts her foot. Claudius
fits the shoe. She turn to him*)
OH WERE YOU EVER STRONGER IN
YOUR LIFE

CLAUDIUS: Never

GERTRUDE: STRONGER
DEEPER
TIGHTER THAN A BOW

CLAUDIUS: Never
Never

GERTRUDE: Me neither
I FLOODED TO MY KNEES
(*They hold a profound gaze. She pulls away and
strides off, trembling, erect...*)

CLAUDIUS: (*Watching her departure*) She cannot walk
straight
She
Her knees
She's all
(*His hand has travelled to his mouth*)
Oh the religion of it
The religion

CASCAN: (*Who has not watched*) I'll call dinner
(*Claudius seems not to hear*)
I'll call dinner
When he doesn't come I'll look for him
First in the stables
After the stables I'll come here

CLAUDIUS: Yes
(*Cascan goes to leave, stops. He looks at the body
on the ground*)

CASCAN: He could not meet her it was sad the way he
could not meet her at the table in the bed this

wandering this travelling but never meeting her I
wonder if it will be the same with you she
changes she is not identical even a sunset might
profoundly alter her a passing cloud perhaps

CLAUDIUS: I meet her
I meet her very well
(*Claudius goes out. Cascan inclines his head in a
bow. The sound of a deep bell*)

3

*Hamlet examines the face of his dead father, formally displayed.
He lets fall the cloth that covers the face.*

HAMLET: I expected to be more moved than this (*Pause*)
Cascades
Storms of
Torrents of emotion
Never mind these things will come later when I
least expect them in bed with a bitch or on a
horse eyes full of tears you're crying she will
say you're crying the horse will neigh yes horse
yes bitch I am and I don't know why I'm blind
I'm choking silly ha ha forgive me ha I'll get off
off the bitch off the horse have you a handker-
chief
(*He laughs briefly*)
Horses don't have handkerchiefs but bitches
might to wipe their crevices that stinks I'll say
that stinks of filthy copulations am I to wipe my
eyes with that yes wipe away and fuck your
finicky fastidious and
(*He laughs, shuddering*)
WOMEN ARE SO COARSE
They are
They are coarse
More so then men
Vastly more
Vastly
I have noticed it
More coarse than men
THE POLITE ONES ARE THE WORST

Behind their downcast eyes these
SWARMING VOCABULARIES
(*Pause*)
Yes
Yes
Certainly I'll cry later
(*Gertrude enters in mourning*)
How did you kill my father I can't work it out
there is no mark on him
(*He looks at her. He laughs*)
I'm crying later
(*He runs to her, clasps her*)
Say you understand I'm crying later

GERTRUDE: Yes
                      Later if you wish
HAMLET: Later
GERTRUDE: Or if you don't wish not at all
                      (*Pause*)
HAMLET: Not at all?
                      (*He seems to consider this*)
                      Yes
                      I had not thought of that
                      The possibility of *not* crying
                      SO ENSLAVED ARE WE BY THESE
                      CONVENTIONS I HAD NOT FOR A
                      SINGLE MOMENT CONTEMPLATED
                      (*He discovers a word*)
                      Tearlessness
                      When
                      Tearlessness might be my way
                      With
                      Death
                      (*He looks at the ground*)
                      Forgive my shocking manners
GERTRUDE: Yes
HAMLET: I hide in shocking
GERTRUDE: Yes
HAMLET: When all the time I think these people are not
                      shocked
GERTRUDE: No
HAMLET: It is so hard to shock them I am failing to shock
                      them look they
GERTRUDE: Yes

HAMLET: ARE UTTERLY UNMOVED
(*He laughs a little*)
When eventually I cease these futile efforts I shall perhaps have passed through the purgatory of adolescence

GERTRUDE: Yes

HAMLET: POSSIBLY
(*He looks at her*)
Or is shocking a career?
A vocation?
A profession worthy of the finest minds?
I don't know
You look so beautiful today
Severe of course
Always severe
When I was a boy a smaller boy I thought why is my mother so severe that face looks chiselled out of stone she is in agony I thought a sort of agony I wish I knew what agony I do know now I know the source of that severity
(*Pause*)

GERTRUDE: You do?

HAMLET: Oh yes

GERTRUDE: You know it and you decline to tell?

HAMLET: WELL YES
I DO DECLINE
MY FATHER'S HERE
(*He pretends to an offence*)
Dear me
Oh dear
Decorum please
Decorum
Now I am king the entire emphasis of government will be upon decorum sitting still for example
HOW FEW PEOPLE CAN SIT STILL (*Pause*)
Only you (*Pause*)
Only you sit still
(*He examines her*)
Knees together
Folded hands
An hour at a time while they
SHIFT

FIDGET
AND FLAP THEIR HANDS
How they must dream
I have often thought this
Of your still white body
How they must dream it jerking like a puppet
under skilful hands
(*He contemplates Gertrude*)
I'm mischievous today

GERTRUDE: You are

HAMLET: My father is to blame
Tomorrow
A different man me
Promise
Hamlet you will say
Stroking my hair
Hamlet
Squeezing my hand
What brought about this shocking alteration
SHOCKING AGAIN
THE WORD
THE IDEA
(*He shakes his head*)
Last day of infancy this
THIS
DAY
THE
LAST
How else could I honour him?
(*He goes to leave*)

GERTRUDE: Shame killed your father
(*Hamlet stops*)
Examine him
Some terrible looking lingers in his eyes
(*Hamlet returns to his father, draws back the cloth
and studies his face. Pause*)

HAMLET: Yes
Yes I see what I had taken to be common agony
is
(*He shrugs uncomfortably*)
I have not seen that many dead
A beggar in December
Some executed felons

And an ancient aunt but he
(*He bites his lip*)
It's horror certainly but
(*He seems to squirm*)
You say
(*Gertrude is about to speak*)
Shh
(*Hamlet moves his position*)
I SEE AN AWFUL ACT FROM UPSIDE
DOWN
(*Gertrude is about to speak. Hamlet puts a finger
to his lips*)
An act which made him wish his life away
Yes
Existence had become intolerable to him
(*He shakes his head as if in disbelief*)
AND I THOUGHT IT MUST BE POISON
I DID
I DID THINK YOU HAD POISONED HIM
(*He laughs, and stops*)
No man dies of poison who does not welcome it
into his veins I know from poisoners
(*He looks up at last*)
You
Choked
Him
With
A
View
(*He stares at her*)

4

Rooks and a graveyard.

GERTRUDE: I met your eyes
I said I would not and then I met your eyes
Up came the laughter
In a wave
I knew it would engulf me so I turned
My shoulders heaved as if hoisted by ropes
I stuffed the handkerchief into my mouth and

Marched
My shoulders heaving and my eyes awash with
tears
Marched
How well I march
No one dares run after me
SHE HAS TO BE ALONE HER GRIEF
COMPELS HER
Admire my skirt
OR SHAME SOME MUTTERED
My skirt says everything to those who can read
skirts
SOME MUTTERED EVEN SHE KNOWS
SHAME
(*She lifts the hem to the knee*)
The bitches with their little life
The dry-arsed hags of loyalty
I FEEL I AM AT SCHOOL (*She laughs*)
Oh
With you I am at school
(*She releases the hem. It falls*)
The uniform was not like this

CLAUDIUS: Nor your cunt either
GERTRUDE: Neither was my cunt now pretend to comfort me
with that oily gravity of heroic relatives I'll walk
a little
Dab
(*She puts the handkerchief to her eyes*)
And
Shake my head
(*She shakes as if grief stricken*)
How good am I?
(*She laughs under her veil*)
HOW GOOD I SEE YOUR COCK ADMIRES
MY PERFORMANCE
Take him out

CLAUDIUS: Out?
GERTRUDE: Now
Out
I have to kiss him

CLAUDIUS: Out?
GERTRUDE: I'll stoop as if
CLAUDIUS: As if what?

GERTRUDE: I don't know why should a widow stoop to grieve of course
(She issues a loud sob, her hands to her face, and tips forward)
Oh give me him to kiss

CLAUDIUS: *(Adjusting his position)* You are
You are
You are so

GERTRUDE: KISS
KISS
(She takes him)

CLAUDIUS: Oh God help everyone
I love you Gertrude God help everyone
(Suddenly he thrusts her away)
OFF
OFF
(He swiftly turns his back, adjusting his clothing as an old woman enters, in mourning, on a stick)

ISOLA: My son's face
I looked at him
Oh what a face
I looked and looked

GERTRUDE: *(Rising)* I could not look

ISOLA: The face was not a king's face where is your king's face I said you look a fool today

GERTRUDE: It was a strange expression certainly I hardly recognized him

ISOLA: And you saw faces on him I expect he never made for others

GERTRUDE: Possibly

ISOLA: Possibly she says he fucked with you I daresay he fucked his own wife surely?

GERTRUDE: Frequently

ISOLA: There are faces come of fucking never seen on ordinary occasions

GERTRUDE: It wasn't one of those

ISOLA: No?

GERTRUDE: Not a fucking face no though they can be quite foolish can they not if one for a brief moment stands aside from if one so to speak climbs out the pool of one's desires dangling one's legs over the side the swimming face there can look foolish

Howard Barker

can it not foolish or worse hateful do you not
find but this face was different this face was a
face I felt of crumpled pride as if some little god
had smacked him
(*Pause. Isola looks at Gertrude*)

ISOLA: Gertrude I lick your hand
I have been a bitch but Gertrude I lick your hand
Gertrude leave my son alone

GERTRUDE: I can't

ISOLA: LEAVE ME ONE BOY GERTRUDE

GERTRUDE: I CAN'T LEAVE HIM ALONE
(*She winces*)
I like you
I have always liked you
But I cannot leave your son alone
(*The old woman turns to go. She stops*)

ISOLA: I saw you as a child once on a wall
Sitting on your hands
Little socks
Your legs swinging

GERTRUDE: Yes

ISOLA: I passed by

GERTRUDE: Yes

ISOLA: And as I passed your eyes met mine

GERTRUDE: Yes

ISOLA: Terrible eyes Gertrude

GERTRUDE: Yes

ISOLA: Terrible eyes and these legs swinging

GERTRUDE: I knew

ISOLA: You knew my mischief

GERTRUDE: Yes

ISOLA: Those legs swinging I knew you knew those
swinging legs

GERTRUDE: And it was you who looked away

ISOLA: I could not tolerate your gaze

GERTRUDE: A child

ISOLA: Humiliated me

GERTRUDE: A child

ISOLA: AND I WAS THE QUEEN
(*She turns to Gertrude at last*)
You
Who was already shameless
Made me ashamed (*Pause*)

Those swinging legs
(*She goes out*)

CLAUDIUS: (*Calling after her*) THEY STILL SWING
THEY SWING TODAY
(*He laughs*)
It's true
You sit on your hands and you
DO IT
DO IT FOR ME NOW
(*Gertrude turns away*)
Gertrude
Do what I say
(*She turns, looks at him*)
Even if you lack the inspiration if it is an empty
gesture women do it all the time don't they they
swallow their indignation in the interests of a
brittle harmony gratify me poor women one
might say gratify me the married ones especially
through gritted teeth they mock desire all right
tomorrow and there's no wall anyway say we'll
play tomorrow little white socks say tomorrow
say
SAY GERTRUDE
SAY
(*A pause. Her looks soften. She kisses him on the
cheek chastely*)

GERTRUDE: She went to a house your mother
A poor house
Nearly every day
A poor man lived there with a crippled wife
Not only crippled also blind
And she cried out
Not your mother
The woman who was blind
OH
OH
I SO WANTED TO KNOW WHAT MADE
THAT CRY SO
OH
AS IF THE EARTH WERE TORN BY
GREAT HANDS OH (*Pause*)
Her ecstasy
Her horror

I don't know which and when she died they
ceased your mother and the poor man (*Pause*)
She took herself to a Dutch musician
A bald man with too many teeth
I KNOW HER HISTORY OH HER HISTORY
(*She shakes her head*)
MY CRY IS NEVER FALSE
(*She glares at Claudius*)
You know that
You know it's never false and if it falters if it dies
I won't pretend it Claudius I will not lie however
wonderful my lying is

CLAUDIUS: Yes
(*She turns*)

GERTRUDE: They are watching us
Like starved birds on a gutter
Heads on one side
They sense the clay depths of our uttering and
hate us for it take my arm now
(*Pause*)

CLAUDIUS: I must have it
(*Gertrude turns to him*)
The cry Gertrude
I must drag that cry from you again if it weighs
fifty bells or one thousand carcasses I must
IT KILLS GOD
(*Cascan appears in mourning and attends discreetly. Claudius alters, and addresses the servant*)
And that is our ambition surely to mutiny is
mundane a mischief which contains a perverse
flattery no killing killing God is our
(*Pause. He goes to Cascan*)
Obviously He rises again
Always He rises
I am not naïve
ALWAYS THIS RISING AND HIS FACE
MORE TERRIBLE EACH TIME (*Pause*)
Tell them we are coming tell them the Queen was
overcome by grief and sought relief among the
graves her sensitivity etcetera her delicacy etcetera let them look upon her stricken face her
shrunken mouth is surely evidence of her despair
it is more thin than newspaper more dry than

newspaper yet all men know yet all men know
yet all men off you go
(*Cascan bows and departs. Gertrude and Claudius
ache, then turn and walk slowly after him*)

5

A dinner. Hamlet, Ragusa and Isola attend. Gertrude enters.

HAMLET:	The skirt's too short
	(*Gertrude stops*)
	However excellent your legs might be
ISOLA:	Shut up
HAMLET:	The skirt's
ISOLA:	Shut up
HAMLET:	Too short
	How long has he been dead my father seven weeks and and
ISOLA:	Shut up you are a bore and a prude
HAMLET:	Make a fool of yourself if you want to
ISOLA:	THERE IS ONLY ONE FOOL HERE AND THAT IS YOU
	(*Pause*)
HAMLET:	Make a fool of yourself and actually your legs are not perfect
ISOLA:	WHAT'S PERFECTION GOT TO DO WITH IT IT'S SEX IT'S SEX SHE'S GOT
	(*Ragusa laughs. Hamlet stops*)
	You are a bore and a prude (*Pause*)
	I hate the word sex I really do I hate the word I tried to shut it out of my vocabulary but frankly it's impossible charm allure sensuality what little words what poor and little words oh God Gertrude (*Gertrude goes to Isola and kisses her cheek*)
	Oh God Gertrude the sex in you
	(*Pause*)
HAMLET:	Surely what's erotic is the skirt?
ISOLA:	IT'S HER
HAMLET:	Being short and so on?
ISOLA:	IT'S HER THAT HAS THE SEX AND YOU ARE

(*She shakes her head*)
He thinks the skirt is sex
(*Ragusa laughs*)
He thinks a short skirt's sex
Oh dear
Oh dear

HAMLET: What a peculiar and disgusting grandmother you are I look at my friends and whilst they may revile their parents they discover in the parents of their parents a refuge from humiliating criticism they can confide they can confess I find this lack in my own life acutely painful it drives me into sordid acts of intimacy I inevitably regret
(*He glares at Ragusa*)
But one must talk with someone
ONE MUST SHOUT ONE'S PAIN INTO A JAR IF ONE HAS NO GRANDMOTHER
(*Pause*)
I'm waspish today (*Pause*)
I'm waspish and still a little infantile I had intended to dispense with it I promised I promised in the presence of my father's body never again would I be infantile but here I am a little still I think a little infantile
(*He hangs his head. Gertrude kisses him*)

GERTRUDE: Hardly at all
HAMLET: Hardly at all thank you (*Pause*)
Your skirt
(*He gestures vaguely*)
Your sex
Your skirt and your sex
EMBARRASS ME
(*He writhes away from Gertrude*)

ISOLA: You are a prig
(*Ragusa laughs, incredulous*)
And a prude (*And laughs*)
And a moralist
(*Ragusa shakes her head with delight*)
And you hide inside your indignation like a baby in a pen
SHAKE YOUR BARS WHO'S LISTENING
STAMP YOUR FEET WHO'S LISTENING

Your mother is magnificent
Too magnificent for you as she was too magnificent for your father
Yes
Yes
He was my son and not yet two months in his grave but still I say it she was too magnificent for him
MAGNIFICENT IS GERTRUDE
All the same she gave birth to a prig
That's God
God must have His little laughter
A PRIG
A PRUDE
AND A MORALIST
Kiss me
Kiss your grandmother

HAMLET: No
ISOLA: (*To Ragusa*) You see
He is a prig
A prude
And a
GERTRUDE: Shh
Shh now
RAGUSA: I love this
I love the way you speak your minds where I come from nobody does it's all politeness obviously the feelings are the same but oh we just go round and round it's a maze it's not conversation
(*Hamlet looks coldly at Ragusa*)
HAMLET: Manners are a maze
Beautiful is the maze of manners
RAGUSA: Is it
I don't think so
(*Cascan enters and bows*)
HAMLET: Ask him
CASCAN: Dinner is
HAMLET: How beautiful the maze is
(*Pause*)
CASCAN: Dinner is
HAMLET: He treads the maze
He treads it in all weathers

	Storms of piss and floods of ordure steaming summers of soiled nakedness still he
CASCAN:	SERVED ON THE LAWN TODAY
HAMLET:	Still he
CASCAN:	Ladies and Gentlemen
	(*Pause*)
HAMLET:	Treads the maze of manners
	I admire him
CASCAN:	I cannot think why the Lord Hamlet should find in me anything to stimulate his admiration
HAMLET:	You see?
CASCAN:	The routine functions of a servant are hardly designed to satisfy the appetites and aspirations of a prince so subtle and refined as the Lord Hamlet is
HAMLET:	You see?
	THE MAZE (*Pause*)
	And yet I think he fucks my mother
	(*Pause, then Hamlet smothers his head in his hands*)
	I'M INFANTILE
	I'M INFANTILE
	Grandma
	Grandma
	(*He extends a pathetic hand. The old woman goes to him, takes him and leads him out. A pause*)
RAGUSA:	Hamlet
	(*She falters*)
	Hamlet is
	(*She shrugs in her embarrassment*)
	I profoundly dislike Hamlet
GERTRUDE:	Yes
	And yet nothing he says is wholly ridiculous is it not even the proposition he has just uttered some of his wildest accusations however random and malevolent if we are prepared to contemplate them seem less preposterous than at first appeared the shock of an accusation so often conceals its insidious attraction (*She laughs*)
	NOW MR CASCAN IS MORE EMBARRAS-SED THAN YOU ARE
	I am abstract
	ALWAYS ABSTRACT

Go down to the lawn Mr Cascan has known me since I was a child and sat in white socks on old walls

CASCAN: Swinging her legs

GERTRUDE: Swinging my legs on walls

(*Gertrude smiles*)

Play with Hamlet and if he spills his food ignore him he does it to offend and eating with his mouth open it's all

Oh

You know my son

(*Ragusa is about to go out when Hamlet bursts in again. He stands, his hand poised to command attention*)

HAMLET: Entering a woman

(*He chews his tongue in his anxiety*)

Being entered by a man

The going in

The coming in

Is

(*He pulls at his face*)

There is love and there is the coming in the coming in and the going in and this

(*He struggles*)

This saves the love from death it is not before the love

(*He grapples*)

There is love and if the love is terrible it runs out of language and in this agony of language this dying of the language the coming in alone can save the love from dying with the language the love which otherwise would howl of wordlessness like a starved dog nailed into a room implores the coming in to save it I am saying the coming in does not come first how can it come before the love implores it how it how it's how

(*They stare at Hamlet, who gazes at the floor in his solitude. His hands knead the air. He turns to go*)

GERTRUDE: Yes

(*He stops, and then goes out*)

Yes

(*In the silence, Ragusa begins to laugh. Failing to smother the laugh, her shoulders heave. Cascan*)

goes out to the lawns. Ragusa lets free the laugh, covering her face with her hands. Gertrude observes her)

RAGUSA: It is impossible to love him
And
He
So
(*She wipes her eyes with her wrists*)
I sometimes go to place my hand on him a gentle hand as if to say stop now a little peace please all this speaking it's not
AND HE SLAPS IT
SLAPS IT AWAY AS IF I PITIED HIM
Touch me I say
There are many ways to know another God gave us hands God gave us eyes why all this speech
MY BRAIN HE SAYS MY BRAIN IS WHERE DESIRE IS
I think that's sad
(*Gertrude looks at Ragusa*)

GERTRUDE: Yes (*Pause*)
Yes (*Pause*)
Yes (*Pause*)
I'm pregnant (*Pause*)
I TELL YOU WHY DO I OF ALL THE PEOPLE I COULD TELL TELL YOU
I suppose because it is a slap this telling
It is a way of slapping you (*Pause*)
Forty-two years old and pregnant I know the day I know the place you do you know you do whole walls in me slid back whole dykes in me were swept away you know what I mean Ragusa it was
(*She stops. She laughs at Ragusa's discomfort*)
You know nothing whatsoever
Wooden in a skirt
Wooden in shoes
And all of your opinion comes from magazines
NEVER MIND I'M TELLING MY CONDITION AND TO YOU
I was so sick this morning
CONDITION
I retched

CONDITION
And retched
CONDITION I CALL IT
This cry came heaving out of me a great dark cry
Ragusa heavy as a spade
MY BEAUTIFUL CONDITION
(*Ragusa stares, afraid*)
You may go now
(*Ragusa goes to hurry away*)
And Hamlet is correct
Desire's
In
The
Brain
(*Ragusa runs out, as Claudius enters. He looks at Gertrude*)
You're late

CLAUDIUS: Am I?
GERTRUDE: AM I AM I HE SAYS AM I LATE
You know you're late
Please don't be late
CLAUDIUS: Forgive me
GERTRUDE: Whilst in itself a little lateness might seem insignificant it is like many things of seeming insignificance deeply significant when added to the rest like uncut nails like unwashed feet flaccid hand-shakes fidgeting in seats the impression of a man is all the bits
CLAUDIUS: Gertrude
GERTRUDE: Taken together
CLAUDIUS: My nails are not uncut Gertrude
GERTRUDE: Please
CLAUDIUS: And I wash my feet
GERTRUDE: Don't
Please
CLAUDIUS: Thoroughly wash my feet
GERTRUDE: Be
Sarcastic
CLAUDIUS: And I am very rarely late
GERTRUDE: You were late yesterday
CLAUDIUS: Yesterday?
Was I?
GERTRUDE: Not very late but late

CLAUDIUS: Hardly late at all I think
GERTRUDE: Hardly late a little late what does it matter how
             late the lateness was you were late
CLAUDIUS: GERTRUDE I WILL SMACK YOUR FACE
             (*Pause*)
GERTRUDE: We are to be in everything immaculate
CLAUDIUS: Yes
GERTRUDE: We are not allowing those who hate us to
             discover any crack or crevice to insinuate a criti-
             cism in
CLAUDIUS: No
GERTRUDE: They will lever us apart
CLAUDIUS: Yes
             I have said I am sorry I was late
GERTRUDE: OH SMACK ME SMACK MY FACE
             (*Claudius hesitates*)
             No don't
             Don't
             Don't
             I cannot go down with a face all
             Can I?
             With a smack?
             (*Pause. Claudius does not strike her*)
             Thank you for wearing a suit
             (*Pause*)
CLAUDIUS: Yes
             Well I
GERTRUDE: How fine you are Claudius
CLAUDIUS: That was the reason I was late I
GERTRUDE: I adore you Claudius
CLAUDIUS: I left in casual clothes
GERTRUDE: Adore you
CLAUDIUS: Only halfway down the stairs did I recall what
             you had said
             To wear a suit
             I hurried back
             I ran darling
             I ran to do your bidding
             Shirts everywhere
             Ties
             Boots
GERTRUDE: Good
             Good

CLAUDIUS: Flinging on and flinging off
GERTRUDE: Good
     Good
CLAUDIUS: Darling I am your hound I am your dog
     (*Gertrude smiles through her tears... His eyes travel over her*)
     That skirt
GERTRUDE: Yes
CLAUDIUS: It's
GERTRUDE: Yes
CLAUDIUS: It's
     (*He thrills to her*)
GERTRUDE: Whatever it is it is for you
CLAUDIUS: Fuck
     Fuck with me
GERTRUDE: No
CLAUDIUS: QUICK
GERTRUDE: No
     (*She holds him with a look*)
     Suffer it
     (*She walks quickly from the room. Claudius is quite still, his gaze fixed on her departing form. Cascan enters with a loaded and unwieldy tray. The sounds of laughter from the lawns*)
CLAUDIUS: I haven't heard it
     (*Pause. Cascan stops*)
CASCAN: Heard it?
CLAUDIUS: Have you heard it?
     I haven't
     Not for weeks
     (*Cascan looks bewildered*)
CASCAN: Heard what my lord?
CLAUDIUS: THE CRY THE CRY OF COURSE
CASCAN: The cry?
CLAUDIUS: THE CRY OF GERTRUDE DO NOT BE OBTUSE
     (*Pause*)
CASCAN: How should I have heard it my lord if you have not?
     (*He makes a slight bow and goes to leave*)
CLAUDIUS: I don't know
     (*Cascan hesitates*)

How should you have heard it if I have not? All the same I have not heard it
(*Pause*)

CASCAN: I must serve the dinner

CLAUDIUS: You must serve it yes
(*Cascan tries to leave for the lawn*)
I HAVE TO HEAR THE CRY YOU KNOW THAT CASCAN DON'T YOU THAT I HAVE TO HEAR THE CRY?

CASCAN: Yes
Yes (*Pause*)
Nevertheless I daresay you would not be gratified if my lady stooped to imitate a thing so rare and reverenced as this exclamation is?

CLAUDIUS: I would not be gratified no

CASCAN: Merely to perform what has been so spontaneous an utterance would compromise the depths of her desire and humiliate her perfect and pathetic nakedness I daresay?

CLAUDIUS: It would
It would humiliate it yes
I REQUIRE THE REAL CRY CASCAN ALL MY LIFE I SOUGHT IT SINCE I WAS A BOY AND PRIOR YES PRIOR TO BOYHOOD IT IS THE CRY OF ALL AND EVERY MOVING THING AND ALL THAT DOES NOT MOVE BONE BLOOD AND MINERAL
Why pathetic
Why *pathetic* nakedness?

CASCAN: All love is pathetic is it not my lord? From the perspective of (*He smiles*)
From the perspective of the universal I was about to say (*Pause*)
I mean of course from my perspective
(*Pause. He declines his head*)
The perspective of a celibate and solitary slave

CLAUDIUS: I don't know (*Pause*)
Yes
Yes it is pathetic possibly (*Pause*)
No
No
Yes
I don't know

I DON'T KNOW IF IT IS
(*Cascan goes to leave*)
The cry is more than the woman
(*Cascan stops*)
The woman is the instrument
But from the woman comes the cry
(*Pause. Cascan bows slightly and retreats*)
And men want kingdoms
Kingdoms
Counties
Forests
Walled estates with speckled deer parks fountains
lakes of trout YOU MAY GO NOW lakes
of trout and ponds of carp OFF YOU GO I
don't require those melancholy proofs of mascu-
linity HURRY CASCAN do I not if I possess
the cry?
(*Cascan has gone. Claudius is aware of his mother in the doorway*)

CLAUDIUS: I'm sentimental
ISOLA: You're a fool
CLAUDIUS: So you say
ISOLA: I do say it
CLAUDIUS: You say it with such frequency it has entirely forfeited its effect
ISOLA: Shut up
CLAUDIUS: And I am not sentimental not sentimental at all I don't know why I said that
ISOLA: Shut up I said
CLAUDIUS: To gratify you possibly
To pander to your prejudices
ISOLA: Claudius
CLAUDIUS: I was late for dinner and now I'm even later
ISOLA: Claudius
Gertrude does not love you
CLAUDIUS: (*Exasperated*) Oh
ISOLA: CLAUDIUS MY SON GERTRUDE DOES NOT
CLAUDIUS: (*Violently*) SO WHAT
SO WHAT
SO WHAT IF SHE LIES TO ME WITH EVERY BREATH
ISOLA: She does

CLAUDIUS: AND OOZING WITH MY FLUID FLINGS UP HER LEGS FOR CRIMINALS TO PADDLE IN SO WHAT SO WHAT
(*Isola turns away*)
SO WHAT IF SHE STOOPS TO SWALLOW DOGS
I do not want this conversation
OR TAKES SYPHILITIC SAILORS AT BOTH ENDS
SO WHAT SO WHAT
I do not want this conversation but you your face your attitude not your attitude your face I really do resent that face which ever since I was a child hung over me like the brass disc of some nagging clock

ISOLA: YOU HAD MORE SENSE AT FIVE
CLAUDIUS: TICK TOCK
ISOLA: THAN YOU DO NOW CLAUDIUS
CLAUDIUS: TICK TOCK
I am concluding this conversation
ISOLA: Conclude it by all means
CLAUDIUS: The conversation is concluded
ISOLA: If you can call abuse a conversation
CLAUDIUS: (*Turning on his mother*) I love the woman
I love
I love
I love the woman
Take my arm now take it let's oh let's be
TAKE MY ARM
(*Isola takes her son's arm. They are quite still. They look over the lawns*)
ISOLA: I live for you my darling son
CLAUDIUS: I know
I do know that
(*A dinner gong is sounded. Claudius goes to obey its call. Isola holds him*)
ISOLA: LET HER WAIT
OH LET THE BITCH WAIT
(*Pause. They hang back*)
CLAUDIUS: (*Going to move*) Now
ISOLA: NOT YET
Oh just look at the
(*Claudius goes to move*)

NOT YET I SAID
(*Claudius is resentful but icily patient*)
Look at the rage on that savage and frustrated
face

CLAUDIUS: I am going

ISOLA: Did you ever see a darker and more vicious face
it's like a wolf's it's like a bat's

CLAUDIUS: GOING I SAID

ISOLA: (*As the gong is beaten ill-temperedly*) A
STOAT
A LYNX
(*As Claudius abandons her and hurries out*)
A CROW
A SHIT-BEAKED RAVEN
OH GO
OH GO

6

Gertrude enters a room. She lifts her skirt above the knee for Isola, showing new stockings.

ISOLA: They're nice
They're nice and your legs are a dream
A dream Gertrude I always thought so (*Pause*)
I said to my boy my poor dead boy I don't like
Gertrude as you know but with legs like those
my liking's neither here nor there is it no mother
he said neither here nor there (*Pause*)
They're wrinkled Gertrude (*Pause*)
On the knee
(*Gertrude looks down at her knees*)
I didn't like you then

GERTRUDE: I did not like you

ISOLA: We did not like each other but
(*As Gertrude tugs the stocking*)
No
No
That's it
We didn't then but now we do you'll kill men
with those legs Gertrude those legs inside those
stockings so what if you're forty-two you'll kill

GERTRUDE: I will
ISOLA: Darling you will
And
Pregnant
As
You
Are
Gertrude
MEN CAN'T KEEP STILL
(*Gertrude laughs*)
They can't
They can't
That friend of Hamlet
Albert Someone Albert Duke of Somewhere
GERTRUDE: Mecklenburg
ISOLA: HIS EYES
HIS HANDS
(*Gertrude laughs again*)
FLUTTER GOES THE DUKE OF MECKLEN-
BURG
(*They both laugh*)
Give him your arse to kiss
(*They cease laughing*)
Your lifted skirt (*Pause*)
Your gaze on the distance like a tethered mare
(*Pause*)
Voices from another room (*Pause*)
Between your buttocks his uneven breath (*Pause*)
At last he rises and his face is wet (*Pause*)
You turn (*Pause*)
He looks up from his knees (*Pause*)
Terrible stare
TERRIBLE STARE
(*Pause. Gertrude is fixed by Isola*)
Albert Duke of
DUKE OF WHERE?
(*Pause. Gertrude moves a little. She examines Isola*)
GERTRUDE: Yes but I love a man
ISOLA: You love a man that's very nice but
GERTRUDE: I love your son
ISOLA: That's very nice but
GERTRUDE: NOT ANY MAN BUT YOUR OWN

ISOLA: GERTRUDE YOU ARE FORTY-TWO (*Pause*)
          And forty-two's not twenty-two (*Pause*)
          It is not twenty-two Gertrude is it?
          (*Pause. Gertrude is shaken*)
GERTRUDE: How strange you are for a mother and not any
          mother but the mother of my lover
ISOLA: The mother of your lover yes but just as forty-
          two's not twenty-two so sixty-two is not
GERTRUDE: (*Bemused*) You are corrupting me
          (*Isola stifles a gasp*)
          I love your son and you
          (*She lifts her hands in disbelief*)
          You are
          You are corrupting me
ISOLA: Those stockings have a fault in them
          (*They exchange a deep stare*)
          Gertrude
          The knees
          Those stockings wrinkle at the knees
          (*Isola urges with a new tone*)
          Gertrude you thrive on men men are your
          ecstasy I was the same I know you watched me
          fuck through infant eyes I do not criticize you
          Gertrude I lavish you I
GERTRUDE: (*Hoisting her skirt and going to unhitch her
          stocking*)
          CHANGE THESE
ISOLA: I applaud your hunger I applaud your greed
GERTRUDE: (*Calling again*) new stockings
          HOW CAN I BE A PROSTITUTE IN
          THESE
ISOLA: Who said anything about prostitutes?
GERTRUDE: (*As Cascan enters*) Clean stockings
CASCAN: (*With a rapid bow*) Madam
ISOLA: You said prostitute not me
          (*Cascan walks out again*)
GERTRUDE: A PROSTITUTE WITH WRINKLED STOCK-
          INGS WILL NEVER
          (*She tears at the suspenders*)
          Now I've laddered them
          NEVER SUCCEED
          So what

So what if they are laddered?
(*She rips at them in her irritation*)

ISOLA: Pleasure is not prostitution Gertrude
GERTRUDE: (*Unhitching them*) Laddered
                Laddered
                AND HIGHER HEELS I'M STOOPING IN
                SHOP DOORWAYS
ISOLA: You're funny
                You're funny but I put it down to your condition
GERTRUDE: CASCAN
                (*She kicks off her shoes*)
                BLUE SHOES
                (*She glares at Isola*)
                Bare legs surely bare legs in blue shoes the stock-
                ings are superfluous?
                (*Isola shrugs, tight-lipped. Gertrude seems calm*)
                I think when you urged prostitution upon me
ISOLA: Darling I never
GERTRUDE: Shh
ISOLA: I never did
GERTRUDE: You little knew my instinct and my inclination
                (*Cascan enters with blue shoes*) for the (*Pause*)
                What?
                What is it? Prostitution?
ISOLA: A profession I suppose
GERTRUDE: A profession thank you COAT
                (*Cascan places the shoes on the floor and goes out.*
                Gertrude, bare-legged, steps into the shoes)
                He'll bring the wrong coat won't he?
                NOT ANY COAT
ISOLA: (*Apprehensive*) Oh dear
GERTRUDE: PROSTITUTE'S COAT
ISOLA: Oh dear oh dear
CASCAN: (*Entering, puzzled*) Prostitute's coat? What sort
                of coat is
GERTRUDE: A COAT SUCH AS A PROSTITUTE WOULD
                WEAR
                (*Cascan is alarmed and swallows hard. His eyes*
                briefly meet Isola's. She shrugs faintly)
                Long
                So it's hidden
                (*Cascan nods, looking at the floor*)
                The belly

So the belly's hidden and the hair
(*He nods again*)
And belted
To draw a line at violation
So whilst I'm owned in one part I'm not owned
everywhere
(*He nods again. He starts to go out*)
And thin
To hint at poverty
(*Cascan goes out. An awkward pause during which
Gertrude stares wildly at Isola, who cannot look
back*)

ISOLA: I'm your ally Gertrude
I'm your
I'm your
(*She shrugs feebly. Cascan enters with a thin, long
raincoat. Gertrude puts it over herself and tightens
the belt*)

GERTRUDE: You see they were already in my wardrobe
The shoes
The coat
The instruments of my vocation
ALREADY THERE
(*She emits a small laugh, and turns to leave. She
stops. Skilfully she reaches under her coat.
She lifts a leg, and produces from her garments
her pants*)
Shan't need those
(*She tosses them to a figure who swiftly enters and
stops. Gertrude marches out*)

ISOLA: IT'S ALL RIGHT
IT'S ALL RIGHT
IT'S ALL RIGHT
SHE'S FUNNY SOMETIMES
IT'S ALL RIGHT

7

*The Duke of Mecklenburg alone, holding Gertrude's underwear
exactly as he had received it. Hamlet enters. He looks. He walks.
He stops. He looks. He prepares to speak. He does not speak. He
plays with utterance.*

HAMLET: She's mad (*Pause*)
           And like the mad embarrassing I'll take those what a
           louche and perverse hospitality you must be think-
           ing in Mecklenburg such things could never or do
           you want them say if you do for all I know you
           might revere the soiled and sordid fragments of
           another's
           SAY ALBERT IF YOU WANT THEM I
           PERFECTLY UNDERSTAND THE (*Pause*)
           I don't understand (*Pause*)
           I do not understand at all why you are clutching
           those ridiculous (*he shrugs*)
           As if
           (*Albert raises Gertrude's pants to his lips and kisses
           them. Hamlet is still and watches, his brows knitted*)
           As if
           (*Albert watches Hamlet*)
           As if
           (*Pause. They stare*)
           At some point Albert I should like to talk of love
           (*Pause*)
           So few ever speak of it (*Pause*)
           And this in spite of OR BECAUSE YES
           POSSIBLY BECAUSE SOME TERRIBLE
           EQUATION MIGHT ACCOUNT FOR IT the
           relentless intimacy of our state the more they fuck
           the less they contemplate
ALBERT: I love your mother and if she's mad good
           (*A pause. Hamlet is exasperated, but patient*)
HAMLET: Love
           Love
           Love my mother?
ALBERT: Help me to sleep with her
HAMLET: Love
           Love my mother
ALBERT: Hamlet
HAMLET: Love her
ALBERT: OTHERS DO (*Pause*)
           The way she stands
           The way she clothes herself
           OBVIOUSLY THEY DO (*Pause*)

                    I'm in such a state of
                    I'M IN SUCH A STATE
HAMLET: Yes
                    Yes you are
                    And if that isn't love I don't know what love is
                    certainly I will intercede for you I will say the
                    Duke of Mecklenburg has been observed inhaling
                    some discarded laundry which bears an intimate
                    relation with you mother
ALBERT: Shut up
HAMLET: With your fundament at least and this is love
ALBERT: Shut up I said
HAMLET: What other word so rarely quoted and refined could
                    adequately describe
ALBERT: Hamlet
HAMLET: His torment
ALBERT: Hamlet
HAMLET: It's love it really is it's
ALBERT: You are diseased (*Pause*)
                    You hate life and you are diseased and however
                    shrewd and ruthless you are in your provocations
                    still you are diseased
                    YES I AM ABSURD
                    ABSURD AND KISS YOUR MOTHER'S
                    PLACE
                    ABSURD
                    ABSURD
                    (*He runs out. Hamlet is still. Gertrude enters and
                    kisses Hamlet on the cheek*)
HAMLET: I'm saying less (*Pause*)
                    Suffering more and
                    (*Claudius enters*)
                    Saying less
                    (*He goes out*)

8

*Claudius sits, his eyes on Gertrude. She feels his gaze. They are
uncomfortable for a long time. At last Cascan enters. He sits. A
pause, as he collects his thoughts.*

CASCAN: Paradoxically (*He strokes his face, a gesture of tact and thoughtfulness*)
            And tragically (*He places the tips of his fingers together*)
            It would appear to be characteristic of passionate love that whilst all the drawers and cupboards so to speak of privacy are flung open and the contents flung about the room in an ecstasy of revelation always an obscurity prevails a locked safe so to speak for which there is no key (*Pause*) In a strange and sinister equation the more we tell the more the untold becomes agony and even that which was once said becomes unsayable (*Pause*)
            Strange
            And
            Probably
            Only
            An
            Aspect
            Of
            Our
            Impenetrable
            Solitude

CLAUDIUS: I've penetrated it I've penetrated her solitude and she mine sorry but we have we did and sorry sorry
            (*Pause. Cascan is patient*)

CASCAN: Lord Claudius can't speak of the one thing he most

CLAUDIUS: I love you Gertrude

CASCAN: He most requires to speak of

CLAUDIUS: Darling I love you (*He lifts his hand in a gesture of apology*)

CASCAN: This is a matter of the utmost delicacy but often it appears the delicate can best be stated by one who if not himself indelicate nevertheless might bring to the subject (*He stops*)
            I mean I can say what others can't (*He turns to Gertrude*)
            Three months apparently and you've made no cry

CLAUDIUS: She has but

CASCAN: You have but these cries whilst reassuring and affectionate lack

CLAUDIUS: Not affectionate

CASCAN: Whilst powerful and urgent

CLAUDIUS: NOT AFFECTIONATE THANK GOD WE ARE NOT MAN AND WIFE

CASCAN: No

CLAUDIUS: Not affectionate
             GERTRUDE SOMETHING'S LOST (*He squirms on the chair. He turns away*)

GERTRUDE: (*Walking pensively, stopping*) I am accused

CLAUDIUS: Not accused

GERTRUDE: Accused and I plead guilty (*Pause*) Not of failing to love I do love

CLAUDIUS: Yes

GERTRUDE: You know the love

CLAUDIUS: I know it yes

GERTRUDE: THE HUNGER AND THE LOVE I FEEL FOR YOU

CLAUDIUS: Yes

GERTRUDE: So I'm not guilty on that score

CLAUDIUS: GUILT I NEVER

GERTRUDE: ON THE SCORE OF LOVE NOT GUILTY

CLAUDIUS: I NEVER SPOKE OF GUILT GERTRUDE (*Pause*)
             You make me feel ashamed (*He lifts his hands helplessly*) You make me feel (*He gestures wildly*) BUT I HAVE TO SAY IT BECAUSE YES BECAUSE OF THE AGONY I SUFFER OVER YOU
             WILL SAY IT
             WILL (*Pause*) Or get it said by some other means
             (*He covers his face with his hands. A pause. Gertrude is infinitely cautious*)

GERTRUDE: Yes
             However
             Yes
             It's true (*She bites her lip. She looks at Claudius*) But do you wish to know the consequences of the fact that what you charge me with is true?

CLAUDIUS: (*Exasperated*) It's not a charge Gertrude

GERTRUDE: IT IS
            IT IS A CHARGE
            AND THE CONFESSION OF IT WILL
            SHRINK YOU
CASCAN: I warned him
GERTRUDE: Yes
            I warn him also
CASCAN: At the time of your husband's death I said
CLAUDIUS: Shut up
CASCAN: This will only
CLAUDIUS: Shut up Cascan (*Pause*)
            Please (*Pause*)
            Cascan (*Pause*) I do know Gertrude I am not
            naïve
GERTRUDE: Never naïve
CLAUDIUS: Never naïve and I know now as I always knew
            your body for all that it's revered by me is flesh
            and being flesh is ground ground trodden
            ground to which I'm bound a dirt poor labourer
            who tills and spills and fights and fails in his
            possession Gertrude it is God I'm fighting when
            I fight in you
GERTRUDE: Yes
            Then you already dread
CLAUDIUS: Yes
GERTRUDE: What I'm now telling you
CLAUDIUS: Yes
            But every dread
GERTRUDE: Is desperate for its satisfaction
CLAUDIUS: Yes
GERTRUDE: The cry's betrayal Claudius (*Pause*)
CLAUDIUS: Betrayal?
GERTRUDE: Betrayal
            And it comes from nowhere else
            (*A stillness overcomes Claudius. He lays his hands
            on his knees. Albert enters and waits, observing
            Gertrude. Isola enters as if from a walk*)

9

ISOLA: You were funny
            (*She goes to kiss Gertrude on the cheek*)

All that about prostitutes (*She kisses her*)
I took you seriously
GERTRUDE: People should
ISOLA: People should?
GERTRUDE: Take Gertrude seriously
ISOLA: Oh she is third person Gertrude is she?
GERTRUDE: Gertrude is
ISOLA: She is and I don't criticize (*She looks at Claudius*)
SON I'M TERRIFIED FOR YOU
(*Pause. Claudius lifts his eyes slowly to his mother*)
Son
Son
God knows I'm trying but you will have to save yourself
(*She turns back to Gertrude*)
(*Referring to Albert*) He's here again (*She nods her head in a conspiratorial way*)
That Duke
That
Where's he from
That boy
He
GERTRUDE: Gertrude's boy? (*Pause*)
ISOLA: Yes (*Pause*)
Him
(*Gertrude turns to Albert*)
GERTRUDE: Mecklenburg
ISOLA: Isn't it peculiar I cannot and I was educated to a high degree I cannot say that word
GERTRUDE: Mecklenburg
ISOLA: Yes
You can say it but not me
I want to say oh anything but that
Middleburg
Magdeburg
But Mecklenburg
OH I SAID IT THEN
(*Her laughter is solitary and brief. She turns to Claudius who ignores her. She leaves, distraught. In the subsequent silence, Claudius rises to his feet*)
GERTRUDE: Speak with Gertrude (*Pause*)

CLAUDIUS: Yes
               (*He lifts his eyes to her at last*)
               Yes (*And goes. Albert laughs*)
ALBERT: Why do you speak of yourself as Gertrude is it
               a form of etiquette the Danish court is so quaint
               in its manners so archaic Hamlet says he wishes
               it were more so and intends to bring back all
               those penalties that have fallen out of use
               regarding for example bowing bowing we have
               entirely abolished I can't remember when I last
               saw anybody bow in Mecklenburg (*He falters.
               Pause*)
GERTRUDE: You must take her from behind
               (*A pause. Albert is dry-mouthed*)
ALBERT: Yes?
GERTRUDE: If you want Gertrude (*He is able to nod*)
               She is pregnant but you must do it from behind
ALBERT: Yes
GERTRUDE: And cover her mouth with your hand (*He nods*)
               Do not kiss her
               (*He shakes his head*)
               Do you understand?
ALBERT: Yes
GERTRUDE: And if she (*She shudders*)
               If Gertrude
               (*To Albert's amazement Gertrude forces her fist
               into her mouth. Her body heaves. Her stifled cries
               come one upon another. At the end of her ecstasy
               Gertrude staggers from the room. Cascan follows
               her, discreetly. Albert is paralyzed. He calls after
               them*)
ALBERT: WHERE?
               WHERE?

10

Ragusa enters a park.

ALBERT: (*Looking at last*) Don't follow me
RAGUSA: I don't follow you Albert
ALBERT: Very well do not contrive to place yourself where
               you know I am likely to appear

RAGUSA: It needs no contriving Albert since you are always in the same place

ALBERT: And is Albert not at liberty to stand in this place or another if he so desires?

RAGUSA: (*Puzzled*) Albert?

ALBERT: How free is Albert?

RAGUSA: What's this Albert?

ALBERT: He regrets profoundly that he kissed you the kiss was spontaneous and inconsequential nothing should be predicated on a kiss of such small significance Ragusa (*He detects a third party*)

Oh look who's here be casual please

Stand further

Look as if

Oh dear oh dear

(*Hamlet enters. He smiles oddly*)

HAMLET: Under the tree (*Pause. Albert looks pale*)

The elm (*Pause*)

If trees could speak oh what a history

I'M SAYING LESS

(*He goes out. Albert squirms*)

RAGUSA: Albert pack your bags

ALBERT: (*Observing a distant figure*) She's here

RAGUSA: Or don't pack them

Don't stay to pack your bags I'll send them on

ALBERT: (*Distracted*) Pack my bags?

RAGUSA: A dozen suits what's that to you the trains leave on the hour

ALBERT: Trains? For where?

RAGUSA: For Mecklenburg

ALBERT: Mecklenburg?

LOOK SHE'S HERE

RAGUSA: Albert

ALBERT: UNDER THE TREE

(*He starts to go to his rendezvous. Ragusa tries to detain him*)

Ragusa I do not know you (*Pause*)

I do know you

Obviously I do know you I know you and I like you but

TRAINS WHAT TRAINS

(*They stare at one another. Albert is earnest*)

Ragusa
The Queen is beautiful and forty-three
Pregnant
Beautiful
And
Forty-three
PREGNANT BY ANOTHER MAN HER HEELS
GOUGE LACERATIONS ALL THE LENGTH
OF ME
It is very exciting very very exciting Ragusa
I am so excited

RAGUSA: Yes
ALBERT: Even the kisses in which I smothered you
RAGUSA: Yes
ALBERT: They too came out of Gertrude's nakedness
I was so proud Ragusa
RAGUSA: Yes
ALBERT: So proud and vulgar that within two hours of seduc-
ing you
RAGUSA: Don't go on
ALBERT: Yes
RAGUSA: Don't go on
ALBERT: A HOUSEMAID AND A WOMAN ON A TRAM
BOTH UGLY
BUT WHAT WAS THEIR UGLINESS TO ME?
(*He laughs*)
Forgive
Forgive (*He turns away*)
She's there
Gertrude under the tree
(*He hurries off. Ragusa stares after him. Cascan is
discovered at the perimeter*)
CASCAN: Miss (*He bows ever so slightly*)
The Lord Hamlet is (*He stops*)
RAGUSA: Yes?
CASCAN: Shh (*He turns his head as if to catch a sound on the
wind*)
RAGUSA: Hamlet is what?
CASCAN: SHH I SAID (*He strains his hearing. There is no
sound*) Forgive me he requests your presence for a
few words only a few words he emphasizes very few
(*Ragusa leaves. Cascan pulls his coat close and sits on
the ground*)

11

Isola enters. She watches Cascan.

ISOLA: Help an old woman at the end of her life
          (*Cascan looks up*)
          Help an old woman no angel but rarely spiteful
kind to her tenants no not always kind two sons
one remaining some secrets some banquets and a
few trips to the war hospitals help her (*He does not
reply*)
I'll beg (*Pause*) I've never liked you (*Pause*)
Never liked you so my begging will probably give
you satisfaction (*Pause*)
I AM BEGGING (*Pause*)
No I'm not I've never begged I don't know how to
do it show me and I'll do it yes I do I begged a man
once don't abandon me I said that's different though
that's love
(*Pause. Cascan is embarrassed*)
Let's have a drink
(*Cascan looks appalled*)
Sometimes it's good to drink with people you
despise (*Pause*)
I don't despise you
(*She is at the end of her tether*)
I do
I do
Of course I do (*She sinks*)
I own estates say if you want them
Furniture
Horses
Pick and choose
I'll walk in rags
I'll die in fields
I'M BRIBING YOU BE BRIBED DAMN YOU
(*She is depleted. Cascan is not cruel*)

CASCAN: Loyalty (*He shakes his head*)
It's comical to you (*He looks at Isola*)
What a painful discovery this was for me who was
taught loyalty to see my masters placed no value on it
(*He stands and brushes down his coat*)
All the same it continued to prevail in me

	An instinct
	An archaism possibly (*Pause*)
ISOLA:	Cascan
	She's bad (*Pause*)
CASCAN:	Your opinion of the Queen
ISOLA:	Not opinion Cascan
CASCAN:	Your opinion even were it proved to be
ISOLA:	BAD IN THE HEART
	BAD IN THE MOUTH
CASCAN:	Not opinion but incontrovertibly
ISOLA:	BAD IN THE WOMB
CASCAN:	A statement of the truth still never could diminish
ISOLA:	AND IN THE CUNT BAD CASCAN
CASCAN:	(*Closing his eyes*) My devotion
	IT'S
	AN
	ECSTASY
	(*Pause. Isola is spent. She tries to lift herself off the ground and fails*)
ISOLA:	Help me up (*Her hand claws the air*)
	Oh help me
	(*Cascan extends his hand and raises her*)
	My boy is dead (*She starts to go*)
	My boy is dead (*She addresses no one*)
	In a war yes such a wicked war the battlefield was in his head
	(*Claudius enters. Isola addresses him as if he were not known to her*)
	Horror
	Unearthly shouts
	And bits of flesh
	THEY FOUND HIM NAKED AND HIS TUNIC RIPPED TO SHREDS AS IF SOME WOLF HAD RAVENED HIM THE SOLDIERS SAID
	Who would do such
	Who would do such
	(*She wanders out, watched by the two men*)
CLAUDIUS:	She was a whore in her own time
	MOTHER
	A whore in her own time yes
	MOTHER

My brother for example
NAME HIS DAD (*Pause*)
MOTHER (*He is distraught*)
I haven't time

CASCAN: No

CLAUDIUS: Not strictly time I do have time time is not in short supply SPACE

CASCAN: Yes

CLAUDIUS: SPACE TO ACCOMMODATE MY MOTHER'S AND

CASCAN: Your own

CLAUDIUS: MY MOTHER'S AND MY OWN (*Pause*)
Yes

CASCAN: Her anxieties on your behalf are perfectly comprehensible but a parent no matter how devoted must appreciate a certain precedence asserts itself in the emotional attachments of a

CLAUDIUS: THE QUEEN'S QUIET CASCAN ISN'T SHE QUIET
My emotional attachments yes
QUIET AS THE GRAVE
Attachments
ATTACHMENTS ASK A SLAVE ABOUT ATTACHMENTS
CHAINS
MANACLES
LOOK A MAN ATTACHED
(He holds up his wrists. He laughs strangely)
i could have you executed for that word
the poverty
the slander
of that word (*pause*)

CASCAN: I intended no offence

CLAUDIUS: To call my agony attachment I say is offence
I'll change the law
As from tomorrow the crime of understatement carries a penalty of death

CASCAN: It was tactless of me I confess

CLAUDIUS: TACTLESS
There you go again
TACTLESS
IT CUT ME TO THE QUICK (*Pause*)

CASCAN: Yes
            Yes
CLAUDIUS: Never mind
            A reptile has a cold vocabulary
CASCAN: I am not a reptile my lord
CLAUDIUS: No
CASCAN: As for executing servants for their choice of words
            I think
CLAUDIUS: (*His hand to his ear*) Shh
CASCAN: The Queen might entertain her own opinion as to the justice of
CLAUDIUS: SHE I SAID (*He glares at Cascan*)
CASCAN: The wind (*Pause*)
CLAUDIUS: The wind yes (*Pause*)
            I'm in such pain
            I'm in such pain
            (*He smothers his head in his hands and rocks from side to side. Cascan observes him for a little while, then discreetly withdraws. Claudius howls*)

12

Gertrude enters.

GERTRUDE: The boy must die (*Claudius looks up*)
            My darling
            My darling
            The boy must die
CLAUDIUS: Yes
GERTRUDE: Kill the boy for rampaging in my belly
CLAUDIUS: Yes
GERTRUDE: For hammering the silence where my child lies
            HE THRUST MY FACE AGAINST THE TREE THE SMELL OF HIS FINGERS AND THE ROUGH BARK SCRATCHED LOOK SCRATCHES ON ME (*She shows her cheek*)
            And cut down the elm
            Whatever its antiquity it must not shelter sheep not sheep or shepherds either
            IT SAW MY NAKED ARSE

COMPLACENT TREE
(*She mocks the elm*)
Men come and go beneath my leaves the lovers
grow embittered their oaths are cast into infinity
fine girls decay and in my shade rotting men
write poetry
SUFFICIENT WISDOM OF THE PASTO-
RAL VARIETY
Call the woodmen
Let it sing in the grate
Let its flames illuminate our white limbs lifting
Bone on stone
Mouth
Floor
Bruising
(*Claudius is thoughtful*)

CLAUDIUS: His fingers
The odour of his fingers you described (*He strug-
gles*)
These fingers closed your mouth presumably or
you could not have smelled them? (*Pause*)
Consequently any cry you made

GERTRUDE: Claudius I did not cry

CLAUDIUS: Would have been smothered would it not?

GERTRUDE: I TELL YOU NO CRY CAME
(*He looks at her*)
How infinitely and passionately

CLAUDIUS: Yes

GERTRUDE: FORENSIC
You are Claudius

CLAUDIUS: Yes
Yes
I could draw from memory the landscape of your
underneath
Volcanic
Oceanic
As it is (*They exchange a look of pained desire*)
Invite him
Tell him under your coat you are undressed
Say but for shoes you are
OH YOU KNOW THE STUFF TO MAKE A
BOY GO ALL

GERTRUDE: I know it yes (*Pause*)

CLAUDIUS: GERTRUDE I COULD MURDER YOU
             MYSELF
             (*They stare*)

13

Hamlet enters holding hands with Ragusa

HAMLET: I'm saying less (*Pause*)
             I'm saying less and the reason I am saying less is
             that speech falters speech flinches when horror
             lifts a fist to it (*Pause*)
             The more horror the less speech I don't say I am
             the first to have appreciated this (*Pause*)
             We're marrying (*Pause*)
             Ragusa is not fit to be my consort she is scarcely
             literate
RAGUSA: I am literate
HAMLET: And my best friend has already (*His mouth goes
             stiff*)
             My best friend having (*Stiffly*) My mother then
             (*He shakes his head*)
             WORDS HOPELESS HERE
             (*He shakes his head more violently*)
             So I am marrying her notwithstanding or (*He
             laughs now*)
             BECAUSE
             BECAUSE
             OF IT
             (*He looks at the floor*)
             You must love the worst you see
             SAYING LESS
             (*He nods his head violently in affirmation*)
             Oh yes
             Saying less (*Pause*)
GERTRUDE: Do you love Ragusa?
HAMLET: No
             No
             Absolutely not the word love has not once con-
             firm this please Ragusa not once passed my lips
             nor will it love I hate it all manifestations of
             the thing called love fill me with horror and

contempt I could elaborate still further but oh I
could speak volumes on this subject but (*Pause*)
I'll write it
I'll write the Book of Love whilst having never
oh not ever loved
(*He bows his head*)
Bless me
Bless me with your poisonous kiss

GERTRUDE: (*To Ragusa*) And you do you
HAMLET: BLESS
(*Gertrude concedes*)
No
She does not love me either
She endorses my analysis

GERTRUDE: (*Frivolously*) The perfect marriage obviously
HAMLET: (*Hurting himself*) I SLAP MYSELF
I SLAP MYSELF
(*Gertrude is horrified*)

RAGUSA: (*To Gertrude*) You are poor-minded
HAMLET: (*Again*) I SLAP MYSELF
RAGUSA: You are belittling and you
HAMLET: SLAP
SLAP
RAGUSA: HAVE NEVER LOVED FOR ALL YOUR
COPULATIONS
HAMLET: SLAP
GERTRUDE: STOP THAT
RAGUSA: FILTH
FILTH
MAN IS BETTER THAN THIS SURELY
FILTH
(*A silence. Ragusa takes Hamlet in her arms*)
Blood
Oh you have hurt your lip
Blood
(*She holds a handkerchief to Hamlet's mouth*)

HAMLET: (*Removing Ragusa's hand*) We are a sacri-
fice
Loveless
Dutiful
And
A
Sacrifice

(*He leads Ragusa away. Claudius looks anxiously at Gertrude*)

CLAUDIUS: Do not be
GERTRUDE: No
CLAUDIUS: I beg you Gertrude do not be
GERTRUDE: No
CLAUDIUS: Humiliated
GERTRUDE: No
CLAUDIUS: Or made to squirm with shame from some
GERTRUDE: No
No
CLAUDIUS: Morally fastidious and finicky
GERTRUDE: Claudius
CLAUDIUS: Shame is our enemy shame alone will spoil us Gertrude
GERTRUDE: I AM NOT ASHAMED
I SHALL NOT BE ASHAMED
WHEN DID I KNOW SHAME
NEVER
AND NEVER WILL I KNOW IT
(*He recoils*)
Do not doubt me Claudius (*Pause*)
CLAUDIUS: Forgive me (*Pause*)
Forgive me Hamlet is
I never speak with Hamlet
Hamlet is
Perhaps I should one day perhaps I (*He smiles thinly*)
Hamlet is your son
(*Gertrude goes to Claudius. She touches his face with profound love. She walks off, and stops suddenly*)
GERTRUDE: But not our son (*She holds her belly*)
NOT OUR SON
(*She strides out, undoing her coat as she goes. Cascan enters*)

14

CASCAN: I find as time goes by as I watch the world from my frankly privileged position
(*He stops, he smiles disparagingly*)

Forgive me I really must articulate sometimes the more curious and paradoxical perceptions that occur to me the rest I promise you I keep strictly to myself (*Pause*)

I find men odder than ever by men I mean the male the male I have because of the unusual circumstances of my life observed from a somewhat zoological perspective (*He laughs a little*)

I am a male myself of course (*He shakes his head*) A male myself and therefore included in my dis-quisition (*He laughs again*)

We prefer the wounds of women to the women (*He shakes his head*)

Why is that?

(*Gertrude enters, doing up the belt of her coat, bare-legged in shoes. Cascan looks at her*)

The Duke of Mecklenburg is on the train (*Pause. Gertrude is shaken*)

GERTRUDE: The train?

CASCAN: The train to Mecklenburg (*He watches Gertrude and Claudius*)

Bags servants dogs and some items of your under-wear I daresay

CLAUDIUS: WHO CARES WHAT YOU DARESAY

CASCAN: Between his fingers as the landscape

CLAUDIUS: WHO CARES I SAID

GERTRUDE: SHH

CASCAN: (*Undeterred*) Slips away blue lakes and yellow harvesting no it's incontrovertible that whilst men scale the fences of desire it's only for the wounds they give they do not actually require to (*Albert enters, breathless with exertion. They stare at him, incredulously*)

ALBERT: I did not mean a word I wrote in that letter

GERTRUDE: Letter?

ALBERT: NOT ONE WORD

GERTRUDE: Letter?

CASCAN: I had not yet delivered your grace's letter

ALBERT: GIVE ME THE LETTER

(*Cascan takes a letter from his pocket. Albert rips it across the middle*)

LIES

                COWARDLY LIES (*He smiles at Gertrude*)
                I WAS ON A TRAIN
                Yes
                RUNNING FROM MY TRUTH I FLUNG
                LIES BEHIND ME (*He laughs*)
                I pulled the communication cord
                Brakes
                Squeals
                Ranting officials
                And
                This spoils it slightly
                Jumping to the ground I twisted my foot
                (*Gertrude laughs. A pause. Cascan leaves.
                Claudius looks at Gertrude and follows him*)
                I've no wish to offend
GERTRUDE: Don't mind him
ALBERT: The Lord Claudius has never harmed me and
GERTRUDE: (*Smiling*) Don't mind him
                (*A pause. Albert is lost for words. He looks at her,
                shaking his head*)
ALBERT: And you are
GERTRUDE: Yes
ALBERT: You are
GERTRUDE: Naked
                Yes
                (*Albert closes his eyes. His hands go to his head,
                which he comforts*)
ALBERT: I cannot describe the exquisite tension you keep
                me in I (*He aches*)
                I almost think
                I do think (*He scoffs*)
                I AM AFRAID TO SEE WHAT I SO WANT
                TO SEE
GERTRUDE: Wait then
ALBERT: WHAT I HAVE SEEN AND HAVE TO SEE
                AGAIN
GERTRUDE: Wait
ALBERT: I AM IN SUCH A TENDER ECSTASY I
                WOULD NOT CARE IF I WERE DEAD IF
                SOME SHOCK STOPPED MY HEART WHO
                CARES WHO CARES
                Say you understand say you know why I stand
                here and do not run like some mad dog to climb

your flesh all mouth and tongue and fists and
(*He aches*)
Say you understand (*He shakes his head*)

GERTRUDE: I'll undo the coat
(*Albert turns from her to avoid the sight. As
Gertrude loosens the belt of her coat she gasps*)

ALBERT: I WAIT
I WAIT
I WAIT

GERTRUDE: Idiot

ALBERT: Yes

GERTRUDE: Oh idiot I am your death

ALBERT: BE IT
BE IT (*He turns violently*)
BE MY DEATH GERTRUDE
(*Gertrude's fingers hesitate at the buttons*)

GERTRUDE: Boy

ALBERT: Boy me
Boy me
STRIP YOU

GERTRUDE: Oh Boy

ALBERT: STRIP YOU I SAID

GERTRUDE: Oh Boy

ALBERT: STRIP
STRIP
STRIP
YOU
STRIP
YOU

GERTRUDE: Boy I (*She gasps again*)

ALBERT: STRIP

GERTRUDE: Love
You
(*Albert goes to seize Gertrude*)
Claudius
(*Gertrude pulls her coat tight over her body as
Claudius enters. Albert is stopped in mid-
movement*)
CLAUDIUS
CLAUDIUS
(*Albert stares at Claudius, who is likewise struck
motionless. They stare, transfixed*)
CLAUDIUS

(*In a brief moment, Claudius fails to murder Albert*)

ALBERT: She
She
(*Seeing Claudius has not acted, he goes to Gertrude and taking her in his arms, kisses her longingly*)
I don't mind death
I don't mind you see
(*He sinks to her knees and embraces her belly*)
NEVER WILL A BETTER MOMENT OCCUR TO ME THAN THIS
(*Claudius sits. Gertrude's fingers idly stroke Albert's head*)
Not if I lived to seven hundred (*Albert sobs*)

GERTRUDE: Get your train now

CASCAN: (*Entering with a timetable*) There's one at midday but it's not (*He turns it round*)
Oh yes it is
It is straight-through
But (*He peers at the small print*)
Lots of stops (*He looks at Albert*)
Probably that won't worry you
What might be experienced as frustration by most travellers will pass unnoticed in that peculiar condition of melancholy which engulfs you now this station that station what's it to you let it crawl until the dawn breaks over Mecklenburg and the conductor under the misapprehension you're asleep is shaking your shoulder we've arrived this is the terminus arrived strange word when your mistress is your white and long-limbed mistress is your pregnant and exquisite queen of forty-three is arrived no that's the wrong word surely?
(*Pause. Albert climbs to his feet*)

ALBERT: Say one word I'll live with you forever
(*Gertrude's gaze falters. Albert goes out. Cascan watches his departure*)

CASCAN: What a fine departure the stupidest individuals I have observed design perfect departures for themselves whereas the sensitive are invariably embarrassing (*Pause*)

Pain ruins their vocabulary (*Gertrude sobs*)
Gestures which might well be efficacious seem to
them facile or false (*She wails. Cascan looks at her*)
They can't win

CLAUDIUS: Do you love him? (*Gertrude shakes her head*)
GERTRUDE ARE YOU IN LOVE WITH

CASCAN: Please that is ridiculous
CLAUDIUS: Cascan I
CASCAN: SO UTTERLY
CLAUDIUS: CASCAN
CASCAN: RIDICULOUS

(*He goes out. Gertrude is quite still, her eyes are
closed. Claudius tries to speak*)

CLAUDIUS: I would have killed Gertrude
(*Gertrude shakes her head*)
Gertrude I would
I would have killed but
(*She shakes her head more fiercely*)
FORGIVE ME WHEN I LOOKED AT HIM I
SAW MYSELF
I saw that
Oh
That
Time-smothering
Self-abnegating
World annihilating
DISBELIEF
YOUR NAKEDNESS WAS MORE INCRE-
DIBLE TO HIM THAN IF GOD STOOD
AND PRESSED THE FIRMAMENT AGAIN-
ST HIS LIPS

GERTRUDE: It is God is it not?
It is God my nakedness?
CLAUDIUS: Yes
GERTRUDE: To you?
It is to you is it?
CLAUDIUS: Yes
Yes
GERTRUDE: AGAIN
CLAUDIUS: Yes
Gertrude
Yes
(*They gaze into one another. They are relieved*)

GERTRUDE: I did not want him dead what is it to me if he
           is dead his body climbed in mine so what
           he might have been a surgeon a surgeon examin-
           ing me and when I looked down at the ground I
           saw his stuff spill out of me it did not cling
           whereas with you I draw it to my depths I
           hoard you I am a fist Claudius a fist retaining
           you
           (*They are enraptured. Then Gertrude frowns*)
           The cry however
           The cry is not kind
           Where there is kindness such as you described
           to me no cry comes so do not say I have betrayed
           you do not punish me I made an instru-
           ment out of my body but you did not play the
           instrument instead of killing you were kind I
           do not criticize but I must wash now I must
           put on plain clothes these high heels and this
           nakedness seem suddenly absurd
           (*She sobs. Claudius goes to act but a gesture of
           Gertrude's stops him*)
           I must be quiet now with my child
           (*A pause. She departs. Claudius is silent, for some
           moments*)
CLAUDIUS: QUIET NOW
           GERTRUDE QUIET NOW
           WHAT IS GERTRUDE QUIET
           (*Cascan passes with a bowl of water and sponge, a
           towel over his arm*)
           Where are you
           (*Cascan stops. Claudius is bewildered*)
           Did you overhear the Queen say she wanted to
           be washed?
CASCAN: I never overhear my lord (*Pause*)
CLAUDIUS: No
           It is an intuition with you is it not an intimacy
           I think should be stopped
           I WILL WASH THE QUEEN
           (*Cascan inclines his head. Claudius takes the
           bowl*)
           I will if anybody does
           (*Claudius goes out*)

15

Cascan meditates. Ragusa enters.

RAGUSA:	You know everything (*Pause*) Don't you? Everything? (*Pause*)
CASCAN:	Yes
RAGUSA:	Advise me then I have such a terror I am doing wrong not to others to myself marriage is the greatest moment in a woman's life to be a bride the day of all days surely and I do not love I do not hate I sometimes pity but love oh love I am betrothed out of a what an impulse of defiance Hamlet calls it faith I don't know I don't know if I (*Cascan makes a gesture of irritation*) share that
CASCAN:	Shh
RAGUSA:	Faith (*Pause*)
CASCAN:	It's not (*Pause*)
RAGUSA:	(*Puzzled*) What?
CASCAN:	The greatest moment of a woman's life
RAGUSA:	Is it not? (*Pause. Cascan watches her*)
CASCAN:	There are two moments of greatness in a woman's life (*He watches Ragusa*) The day on which she gives birth
RAGUSA:	Oh yes certainly (*Pause*) And the other?
CASCAN:	The day on which (*Pause*) Out of a terrible hunger (*Pause*) She lies to her husband
RAGUSA:	Hunger?
CASCAN:	For another man now miss be kind enough to note that nothing I have said may be constructed as advice a servant does not give advice albeit he knows everything advice is cheap service is (*He smiles*) not cheap
RAGUSA:	No Not cheap at all But rare and oh I wish Hamlet had you for his oh

	Hamlet should have you
CASCAN:	I could not serve the Lord Hamlet
RAGUSA:	No you are the Queen's and (*She shrugs*)
CASCAN:	Great is the Queen Gertrude
	Great is the Queen
	(*Pause. Ragusa goes to leave*)
	Her life is such a seeking and so beautiful is her pain (*Ragusa stops*)
	How could I not relieve her?
	It is a passion in me and a faith
RAGUSA:	Yes (*She bites her lip, frowns*)
	And my life is poor
	(*She sobs and runs out*)
	SO POOR MY LIFE

16

Gertrude's cry. Cascan hurries off.

HAMLET:	(*Entering*) Disgusting
	(*The cry*)
	Disgusting
	(*The cry*)
	Disgusting
	Disgusting
	Disgusting
	(*The cry*)
	DEGOUTANT
	DEGOUTANT
	ABSOLUMENT DEGOUTANT
	The woman I decline to employ a word like mother biologically correct though it might be the woman (*The cry*)
	DEGOUTANT
	ABSOLUMENT DEGOUTANT
	Is 43 and by the laws of nature if nature were not so contaminated with disease should have shed her last egg whole easters and christmases ago this faded and
	(*The cry*)
	DEGOUTANT JE DIS
	should be seated in a rocking chair with black

	blankets spread across her knees
	(*An infant's cry. Hamlet is stock still. Isola hurries in*)
ISOLA:	It's alive
	(*And hurtles out*)
HAMLET:	Deformed surely his lip disfigured by a sneer of such a magnitude it stands before his vision like a wave so when she goes to raise him to her shrivelled breasts she sees
ISOLA:	(*Hurrying back again with a mass of linen*)
	It's perfect and a girl
	(*She hurries out again*)
HAMLET:	Her filth repudiated PERFECT IN WHAT SENSE repudiated by the howling product of her delinquencies PERFECT IS A DEAD MAN'S QUALITY
	(*He laughs, he sniggers. Claudius enters*)
CLAUDIUS:	Your sister smiled
HAMLET:	(*Turning*) Smiled did she who would not smile to have escaped the fetid dungeon of my mother's womb the thing was rinsed in torrents of
	I SHAN'T GO ON
	Flooded with the fifth of
	I SHAN'T (*He purses his lips*)
	I'm saying more you notice this was unavoidable if I were not to develop incurable erosions of my bowel I bled some mornings but since I was restored to ranting this haemorrhage has stopped
	I SHAN'T HOWEVER SAY MORE OF MY MOTHER'S STINKING FUNDAMENT ALBEIT MUCH MORE COULD BE SAID
	(*Claudius glares at Hamlet*)
CLAUDIUS:	I say it
HAMLET:	You say it yes
CLAUDIUS:	The more that could be said
HAMLET:	Yes
CLAUDIUS:	I say it
HAMLET:	Yes
CLAUDIUS:	I say it and I say it
HAMLET:	You say it and say it yes
CLAUDIUS:	I say it and I say it and I say it again
HAMLET:	You do yes
	(*Pause. Their eyes hang on one another's*)

	If God meant cunt to be religion I think He would not have situated it between a woman's legs would He?
ISOLA:	(*Entering in delight*) She is ADORABLE
HAMLET:	By piss and shit would He?
ISOLA:	Adorable AND WITH MY EYES SO GERT-RUDE SAYS
HAMLET:	Hidden from the sight of men and yet further smothered in a forest what could that intend
ISOLA:	I am going to be silly so silly about this child I warn you
HAMLET:	But to confirm its sordid function
ISOLA:	AND WHY SHOULDN'T I?
CLAUDIUS:	Function?
ISOLA:	My first grand-daughter isn't she?
CLAUDIUS:	Function he says
	FAITH COMES FROM SECRET PLACES AND IN THE DAZZLING CATHEDRALS OF LIGHT IT DIES
	(*For the first time he removes his eyes from Hamlet*)
	Show him his cousin or his sister is it let him see the function's functioning
	(*Hamlet goes to leave with Isola*)
	SHE CRIES
	Not the child the mother
	She cries for me
	(*Hamlet looks back*)
	IN MY MOUTH SHE SAYS
	ANYWHERE
	BUT ENTER ME
	(*Choking his resentment, Hamlet leaves with Isola. Cascan, in an apron, is discovered*)
CASCAN:	Not wise
CLAUDIUS:	He maddens me
CASCAN:	Not wise I said
CLAUDIUS:	LET HIM PLOT MY EXECUTION
	LET YOU
	LET ANYONE (*Pause*)
CASCAN:	Your death would be regrettable
CLAUDIUS:	Is that so?
CASCAN:	Insofar as it would devastate my lady (*Pause*)
	Sufficient reason I suggest to refrain from fuelling

her son's resentment
(*Claudius looks critically at Cascan*)

CLAUDIUS: Her cries I thought peculiarly similar to those she utters in the act of love yet this was pain surely?

CASCAN: The Lord Hamlet

CLAUDIUS: Of course birth pain might be an ecstasy or conversely yes we must consider this it might be agony for her to love the agony which comes from a mortality she longs to shed and which

CASCAN: The Lord Hamlet

CLAUDIUS: I AM A STUDENT OF HER SOUNDS

CASCAN: IS KING HERE NOW (*Pause*)

CLAUDIUS: The king governs the kingdom
Gertrude governs me
To him the armies and the acres
My whole life's in her belly in my opinion a superior estate

CASCAN: (*Cascan frowns*) Yes
Yes
But those who rule us hate one woman's womb even to lie beyond their dispensation
(*Claudius looks puzzled*)
The police

CLAUDIUS: The police?

CASCAN: Are posted even there
(*Claudius frowns*)
How little my lord understands of the ambitions of the moralists
(*With a resigned air, Cascan goes to leave. He suddenly stops in his tracks*)
You must murder Hamlet
(*Cascan squirms*)
I have usurped my service
I have broken with my faith
Never did I state a solitary objection nor initiate a course of action never recommended or uttered one word of dissent
A SERVANT MAY NOT URGE (*Pause*)
I preserve my mistress and that is my defence
(*Claudius is shaken*)

CLAUDIUS: Hamlet is the Queen's son

CASCAN: The stronger his passion to torture her

CLAUDIUS: Torture her?

	She is his mother
CASCAN:	He will burn her at the stake
CLAUDIUS:	Cascan
CASCAN:	IT WILL DEMONSTRATE THE AUTHEN-

TICITY OF HIS CONVICTIONS

Oh

Oh you do not know the moralists you do not know the python length of their ambition and how could you innocent oh innocent are the immoralists I must wash your tragic daughter

(*He goes to leave*)

What is her name?

(*Claudius shrugs*)

Oh

Lend her a name if only to identify her grave

CLAUDIUS: You choose

(*Cascan sweeps out but is obliged to step back to make way for Gertrude who enters holding a pair of high-heeled shoes in one hand and with the other pulling a gown around her nakedness. Cascan and Claudius watch as Gertrude drops the shoes to the floor and controlling her frailty, steps into them. She proceeds to remove a lipstick from her pocket and with infinite will, colours her mouth. Cascan suffers. Claudius exults. With a triumphant gesture Gertrude tosses the lipstick far away*)

GERTRUDE: MUTINY (*She laughs*)

I MUTINY

(*She staggers. She grasps. The child cries*)

Drink me Claudius

Let my daughter queue

(*Gertrude opens her gown at the breast. Claudius goes to her, kneels, suckles her*)

CASCAN: (*Discreetly turning away*) I like Jane myself

I like the single syllable

As if a clock on a high tower chimed but only once

(*Gertrude shudders in her ecstasy, her hand cradling Claudius's head. Ragusa, hurrying in, is staggered by the spectacle and fixed to the spot*)

Do you like Jane Miss?

(*Ragusa's hands flutter in her speechlessness*)

My mother gave me such a foolish name I have

never dared reveal it
(*She runs out*)
Perhaps it satisfied her thinking how I'd squirm
to speak it but I don't I don't speak it and now
she's dead of course
(*Claudius ceases. Gertrude covers herself. The
child bawls*)
No one knows it now
(*Gertrude sits*)
Unless
And this I deem unlikely
Some official in the registry has selected it from
among the most preposterous to act as an
admonishment to thoughtless parents yes let's
say Jane let's spare the child one cause for resent-
ment
(*Hamlet enters holding the bawling infant in his
arms and rocking it*)

HAMLET: (*As if charmed*) Sucking my finger
Yes
I am perhaps her brother but is it love I don't
think so myself (*He laughs*)
Ragusa has laid a complaint against you mother
AGAINST THE QUEEN
SILLY I SAID
But all the same it has to be investigated that is
the law the most humble and despised among the
citizens can call their betters to account
A LAWYER WON'T TAKE LONG TO
THROW THAT OUT
Ow
She sucks like a calf
But is it love I don't think so myself
No
Infants are not sentimental what they require is
blood
DID I SAY BLOOD
I must mean milk
(*Hamlet offers the baby to Gertrude, who makes
no move to take it*)
Ragusa's complaint
SILLY GIRL SHE WILL BE RIDICULED IN
COURT

Concerns the welfare of an infant
(*He offers the child to Cascan instead. Cascan takes it*)
Which I suppose must be the business of the state as warfare is as gardening is as is the painting of the frontier posts (*He laughs*)
Are they not the inheritors of the earth and all our labour is it not directed to the enhancement of existence for the newly and the as yet un
THE NEWLY AND THE AS YET UN?
(*He frowns. He goes to Gertrude*)
You have got lipstick on your teeth
(*He stares at her, turns swiftly and goes out. Cascan yells at Claudius*)

CASCAN: KILL HIM
KILL HIM
KILL HIM
QUICK
HE'S ON HIS OWN
HE'S UNACCOMPANIED
KILL HIM
KILL HIM
KILL HIM
QUICK
(*Claudius looks from Cascan to Gertrude, hesitant. Cascan, boiling with impatience, races after Hamlet holding the child in his arms*)

17

Isola enters with the infant in her arms.

ISOLA: Jane
Oh
Jane
AUSPICIOUS THIS
An hour old or is it less an hour in the world and
I'M NOT CLAIRVOYANT BUT
Jane
Oh
Jane
TWICE DRENCHED IN BLOOD

(*Claudius races from the room*)
That is auspicious darling
I'M NOT CLAIRVOYANT BUT
TWICE RINSED IN BLOOD

GERTRUDE: Shut up or I'll smack you
ISOLA: TWICE GERTRUDE
TAKE HER FROM ME
TWICE RINSED IN BLOOD
GERTRUDE: Whose?
Whose blood?
ISOLA: TAKE HER
GERTRUDE: (*Refusing*) WHOSE BLOOD I SAID
(*Pause. Isola stares, shakes her head*)
ISOLA: I saw him running
Babe in arms
And with his apron on
Flapping
Flapping apron
And these shoes with the steel tips on
Sliding
Slipping
Whereas Hamlet's shoes are soft
Down steps
And skids
THE KID I SAID
A miracle
He never tripped
These shoes with the steel tips on
Clatter
Clatter
The noise
A regiment
But Hamlet's lost in thought
He never flinched
The servant grabs him round the neck
THE KID I SAID
With one arm round his neck he pulls him back
One arm
The other
Well
Jane's in that
And tries to choke him
All this in silence

Yes
The kid's asleep
He could have dropped her
But he hung on
His face white as a sheet
He isn't strong
No
Hamlet's stronger
But also Hamlet has a knife
So strength's nothing to do with it
THE KID I SAID
And sticks it in
Once
Twice
The servant drops
Not drops
He doesn't drop he sinks
Holding the kid
He sinks
AND HAMLET JUST GOES ON
OH HAMLET
HAMLET JUST GOES ON
I think
Oh more than necessary
I really think
And all the time Jane is asleep
It isn't noisy
The servant
I never liked him
The servant doesn't speak
Or moan
Or
Anything (*Pause*)
The blood was (*Pause*)
Oh the blood (*She shakes her head*)
I washed it off
I washed it off the kid and put her in clean things
The path however
OH THAT AWFUL PATH
(*Pause. Gertrude is still*)

GERTRUDE: My daughter please
(*Isola hands over the child. She hesitates*)

ISOLA: He should have dropped her

It doesn't hurt to drop a baby
Even on its head
They're soft
You and I
We know babies don't we
But him I don't think he had ever touched one
(*She shrugs*)
To kill someone you must have two hands free
(*Pause*)
I would have thought
(*She goes out. The infant makes small and anxious
sounds. Slowly, absently, Gertrude loosens her gown
at the breast*)

18

She turns her back, and feeds. Claudius enters.

CLAUDIUS: Forgive me
(*Gertrude neither moves nor speaks*)
Forgive me (*Pause*)
Forgive me (*Pause*)
I DON'T KNOW WHAT FOR GERTRUDE
BUT I APPEAR TO NEED FORGIVING
(*She is silent and still*)
Possibly I don't (*Pause*)
Possibly I don't require forgiving possibly I
have merely as so often in our history detected
in your manner how extraordinary this is in
your ABSENCE OF A MANNER EVEN that
I have somehow by some slip some over-
sight some negligible omission contrived to
injure you
(*Gertrude turns and studies him*)
GERTRUDE: I
CRY
YOUR
CRIME (*Pause*)
CLAUDIUS: Yes
Yes
I know you do

(*He frowns. He turns to go*)
I'll poison him

GERTRUDE: POISON
POISON WHO
(*Claudius stops*)

CLAUDIUS: The king your son I'll

GERTRUDE: POISON WHO
(*She appears horrified. They comprehend one another. Claudius leaves. Ragusa hurries in*)

RAGUSA: THE CHILD'S REMOVED

GERTRUDE: Remove her

RAGUSA: The welfare of the child must be of paramount consideration in all issues of

GERTRUDE: REMOVE HER THEN

RAGUSA: (*Stepping forward briskly and snatching the infant*)
The unseemly haste with which you concede possession of your daughter confirms our doubts as to your suitability for parenthood

GERTRUDE: Her name is Jane
But that was in her first life
(*She turns to call Cascan*)
BRING ME MY (*Pause*)
He's dead
MY BLACKEST AND MOST
He's dead
MY WORST BLACK
Dead now
Dead now (*Pause*)
He sponged me
Oh yes
My servant sponged me
Lovingly
Between my legs
Between my breasts
(*Ragusa stares in disgust. She turns to go*)
I DON'T KNOW WHERE MY THINGS ARE
(*Gertrude half-laughs*)
He did the wardrobe
I DON'T KNOW WHERE MY THINGS ARE
AND I'M NOT DRESSED
(*Ragusa hastens away. The child cries bitterly*)

19

Hamlet enters, wearing Cascan's clothes.

HAMLET: The world is full of things I do not understand
            but others understand them evidently for
            example shoes those shoes have heels of such
            extravagant dimensions how can you move
            except by dislocating your entire anatomy it is
            as if you held your body in contempt as if you
            found your shape unsatisfactory shoes are a con-
            sequence of nature certainly of cold and winter
            but should shoes not enhance the action of our
            limbs should they not encourage us to act in
            sympathy with the body's functioning not trick
            us into grotesque parody the world is full of
            things I do not understand but others under-
            stand them evidently
            (*He passes around Gertrude, studying*)
            By this perverse and extreme elevation of the heel
            your posture is so tilted by the shift of gravity a
            stranger unacquainted with our habits would
            howl with ridicule I look at athletes how beauti-
            fully they move and always in such harmony
            whereas women who have lived in these they
            stagger on their swollen joints and damaged
            knees the world is full of things I do not under-
            stand but others understand them evidently
            (*Pause*)
            Be barefoot now
            (*His eyes meet hers. She is adamant*)
            REMOVE
            THE
            UNMATERNAL
            CLUTTER
            CLINGING
            TO
            YOUR
            FEET
            (*She stares, unmoved*)
            For
            The
            Morally

Offended
Amputation
Is
Always
The
Last
Resort
(*Gertrude is defiant. With a gesture of self-assertion she slips the gown from her shoulders and lets it fall to the floor. She is naked before Hamlet. His gaze does not falter*)
The world is full of things I do not understand
(*He senses the presence of a third party*)
But others understand them evidently
(*He turns to see Claudius, holding a glass of wine. The sight causes Gertrude to catch her breath. The sound alerts Hamlet, who looks to her again. His mind works. He looks back and forth. Gertrude gasps, her hand to her mouth*)
I am the servant
Surely
Therefore
I
Should
Serve
The
Drink?
(*He goes to collect the glass, his hand extended*)

CLAUDIUS: (*With a bow*) The King is not the Servant
He
Merely
Wears
The
Clothes

HAMLET: I
Ape
His
Excellence
(*Claudius relinquishes the glass to Hamlet who goes to carry it to Gertrude*)

CLAUDIUS: Gertrude
(*Hamlet stops*)
Do

	Not
	Drink
	(*Pause. Hamlet calculates*)
HAMLET:	Don't drink?

For whom then is the drink intended or is the drink your own forgive me oh I have in an excess of manners confiscated yours
(*He goes to restore the glass to Claudius, who does not take it*)
Please
Your
Glass
Of (*Pause*)
YOUR
OWN
GLASS (*Pause*)

GERTRUDE: You drink it
You drink his glass
(*Hamlet looks over his shoulder at Gertrude*)

HAMLET: I
Drink
His
Glass?
I
Hamlet
Drink
The
Glass
Of
Why (*Pause*)

GERTRUDE: I don't know
I DON'T KNOW WHY JUST DRINK THE
(*Her hands lift*)
I don't know why

HAMLET: One would think
Oh
Silly but
(*He shakes his head*)
So many things I do not understand but others understand them evidently
WHAT IS IN THE GLASS THAT I SHOULD
(*Neither Gertrude nor Claudius speaks. On a sudden impulse Hamlet lifts the glass to his lips and*

swallows the contents. Gertrude shudders. Her cry heaves out as Hamlet staggers. Claudius exults)

CLAUDIUS: Gertrude
Gertrude
(Her cry heaves out again. She holds herself as if she were terrified of her own disintegration)
Gertrude
KILLING GOD
(He is transfixed by her ecstasy. Hamlet sinks to his knees, the glass unbroken in his hand, his eyes on his mother. Again she heaves out her cry)

GERTRUDE: I CAN'T
I CAN'T
(Her hands move as if she were grappling an invisible opponent)

CLAUDIUS: Gertrude
GERTRUDE: OH STOP
OH STOP
(Again her cry comes. She is doubled. Still Claudius observes her. Hamlet, by his final exertion, stands the glass on its foot, an action of perfect will. He dies. Only now does Claudius go to Gertrude. He wraps her in an embrace of exquisite tenderness. They remain thus, a trio of extinction as Isola enters pushing a pram. She stops, observing the scene, and on tiptoe is about to leave again when the child cries. She stops. Claudius and Gertrude end their embrace)

ISOLA: I heard this
I thought
I heard this
I thought
(She shrugs with terror, embarrassment)
NEVER MIND WHAT I THOUGHT
(She wants to move off)

CLAUDIUS: Don't go
ISOLA: I want to
CLAUDIUS: Don't go Mother
ISOLA: I WANT TO
I WANT TO THOUGH *(She seems fixed to the spot)*
Shops
Sugar

Loaf
Shops
Loaf
Gertrude
(*She falters as Gertrude walks unsteadily towards her and with a wail falls into her arms. Isola is stiff, horrified. Gertrude's tears cease. She removes herself. She gazes at the floor*)

GERTRUDE: My bladder
My ovaries
My bowel
This rushing in them as a storm in gulleys washes washes
My kidneys
My belly
My womb
The rivers boiling through
Latin names now
Urethra
Vulva
Mammary
Surging as the blood goes flooding more blood than any body can contain
The brain however
THE AGONY OF BRAIN (*She stares at Isola*)
Go shopping now you rightly have discerned your own extinction chalked on the wall
Go shopping and in the market say I won't pay that
Preposterous price say for a kilo of
ANYTHING THAT WILL DELAY YOUR HOMECOMING
(*She looks at the pram*)
How I love a pram a pram pushed and the dormant child between great bags of groceries washing powder and the bus queue bleach and the tram
(*Biting her lip with apprehension Isola swiftly departs with the pram. Gertrude is still*)
Strip my son now of his clothes his clothes that were not his and stretch him naked somewhere
HOW BADLY HE REQUIRED THOSE CLOTHES

CLAUDIUS: Yes
GERTRUDE: But do not clean them
CLAUDIUS: Clean them?
         No
GERTRUDE: NEVER TO BE CLEANED THOSE CLOTHES
         (*Pause. Claudius is about to move to embrace Gertrude but she stops him with a look*)
         The cry
         The cry
CLAUDIUS: Bigger
GERTRUDE: Bigger
         Yes
         BIGGER THAN MY BODY CLAUDIUS
CLAUDIUS: Yes
GERTRUDE: (*Horrified*) MY WALLS WERE FALLING
CLAUDIUS: Yes
GERTRUDE: MY LIMBS CLAUDIUS
         MY HEAD
         IN ALL DIRECTIONS
CLAUDIUS: Yes
GERTRUDE: I DID NOT THINK
         AT THE CRY'S END
         I COULD BE STILL INTACT
CLAUDIUS: Yes
GERTRUDE: CLAUDIUS
CLAUDIUS: (*Exulting*) Yes
         (*She shakes her head, seeing he does not know her horror*)
         And you were not fucked (*Pause*)
GERTRUDE: Your eyes
CLAUDIUS: My eyes yes
GERTRUDE: I was eyed
         EYED WAS ENOUGH
         (*Ragusa enters. She stares at the body of Hamlet. They seem unaware of her*)
         DON'T ASK ME
         OH CLAUDIUS DO NOT ASK AGAIN
         (*She stares at him, a plea. He defies her. She walks out*)
RAGUSA: (*Her eyes not shifting from Hamlet's body*) Poor woman take her to bed
         (*Claudius is puzzled, but turns to go*)
         I'll be there however

(*He turns. She laughs shrilly*)
I'LL BE IN THE BED
(*She looks at him*)
NO-LAW BECOMES LAW THEREFORE I
MUST BE
(*She makes a gesture*)
I
I
I (*She smiles*)
ALREADY YOU BETRAY HER
(*Claudius goes to take a step towards Ragusa and
stops. She taunts him with a laugh, shaking her
head*)
ALREADY I AM IN THE BED
(*Ragusa goes out. Claudius is thoughtful. He goes
to Hamlet's body. He starts to remove Cascan's
suit but stops*)

CLAUDIUS: Oh poor unloved
Oh
Poor
And
Never
Loved
(*He tries to strip the Jacket*)
I'm crying
Yes
I'm crying (*He tugs*)
Me (*He stops*)
And why not why not me poison notwithstand-
ing why not me (*He points*)
THAT WAS YOUR WIFE
Oh
Poor
And
Never
Loved
YOUR WIDOW WANTS TO SHUDDER
UNDER ME (*He shakes his head*)
That Cascan
That Cascan he (*He returns to his task*)
No wonder you paraded in his clothes like some
champion flourishing a trophy
HE WATCHED WITH SUCH

I resented it
We both did
You and me
With such
THIS COLD WATCHING AND
(*He stops to recollect*)
He made me feel turned on a wheel and dirty as if
some oily rain fell on a mask a grinning thing a
fairground object brass or peeling paint my life
and my desires HOW I WISHED TO SAY THIS
BUT I NEVER DID are REAL
Ha
Ha
THIS COLD WATCHING
(*Gertrude has returned and waits. She is impeccable, funereal*)
I have the jacket (*He holds it out in one hand*)
The trousers I

GERTRUDE: Shh
CLAUDIUS: Haven't yet
GERTRUDE: Shh I said
(*He climbs to his feet. They exchange a long look*)
CLAUDIUS YOUR DEATH IS NEXT (*Pause*)
I shuddered when I knew it I SAY DEATH I
MEAN SOME WRITHING MURDER call it
death (*Pause*)
Not today not imminently today is grief today is
silent walking and staring in the pool of memory
terrible reflections in the pool and self-disgust
the womb a shrunken thing in masonry the
(*sighs*) all chalk and mouth a cave of dust
another day however

CLAUDIUS: Yes (*Pause*)
GERTRUDE: Oh do you know it yes you do you know it too I
shuddered when did you know how long have
you
CONCEALED YOUR (*She glares*)
I COULD STRIKE YOU

CLAUDIUS: I love you
GERTRUDE: I COULD STRIKE YOU
(*She sways. A pause. Her hand rises and falls*)
My darling
Get out of my sight

My darling
GET OUT OF MY SIGHT
(*Claudius leaves*)

20

Albert enters in mourning.

ALBERT: I came at once
               (*Gertrude turns. Albert folds his hands in front of
               him and stares at the floor*)
               And that wasn't soon enough for me
               THANK YOU DEATH
               THANK YOU DISEASE (*He bites his lip*)
               Poor friend
               Poor friend but was he
               Sitting on the train I thought was Hamlet any-
               body's friend
               It isn't him I'm here for is it Gertrude I am here
               for you
GERTRUDE: Our pleasure in the Duke's return is inevit-
               ably diminished by the circumstances in which
               we
ALBERT: Tip Hamlet in the river and let the river wash
               him to the sea let cod pull Hamlet in a hundred
               pieces dead or alive he's nothing to me am
               I coarse so are my feelings when I look at you I
               dream your arse I dream your legs wide open
               and my tongue already aches with anticipation
               of the deep searching it will do
               (*Ragusa enters in mourning*)
               Ragusa (*He goes to her*)
               Ragusa
               Poor Danes
               Poor Denmark
               And poor you
               (*They embrace formally*)
RAGUSA: He had so many plans
ALBERT: A more fertile brain I never knew
               (*Claudius enters with Isola. Albert goes to them
               and kisses the hand of Isola*)
               Is it not true he had commissioned architects to

	rebuild Elsinore in glass?

RAGUSA, ALBERT and the rest speak:

	rebuild Elsinore in glass? Why glass?
RAGUSA:	It is transparent
ALBERT:	Quite so It is defined by its transparency
RAGUSA:	(*Looking at Claudius*) All acts of love he wanted under public scrutiny Lying Darkness Secrecy Hamlet abhorred
ISOLA:	It started off with curtains (*They look at her*) Down came all the curtains Then he had the workmen take the locks off all the doors Then it was the doors IT'S DRAUGHTY HAMLET I SAID (*She* *chuckles fondly*) Better you freeze he said than love is spoiled by (*she stops*) WHAT IS THAT WORD? HE USED IT ALL THE TIME
RAGUSA:	Clan – destine
ISOLA:	That's the word CLANDESTINE Better you freeze than love is (*She stops*) Poor boy Poor boy because it is (*Pause. The infant Jane is heard to cry offstage.* *Isola hurries off to attend. Gertrude takes the few* *steps to Hamlet's body*)
GERTRUDE:	A killed child on the floor and in the corridor another famishes AND YET I AM MATERNAL
RAGUSA:	Go to her
GERTRUDE:	No It's stopped It's stopped (*The child is silent*) How necessary it flatters us to think we are and how terrible it is that we are never necessary

KISS ME
LIFT MY VEIL AND KISS ME

RAGUSA: THIS IS MY HUSBAND'S FUNERAL (*She seethes*)
Please
Please

GERTRUDE: (*Deliberately*) ALL RIGHT I'LL LIFT IT
(*She throws aside the veil and waits*)

RAGUSA: Please (*She looks to Claudius*)
And please again
(*Claudius hesitates. Albert seizes the initiative and kisses Gertrude on the mouth. He steps back. Gertrude looks at him*)
How it gratified me when I came here
The sheer saying
What liberty
The sheer saying
The thought straight to the mouth
And no queuing
No queuing up behind behind the teeth
OUT THOUGHT
OUT INJURY (*Ragusa laughs strangely*)
AND GERTRUDE FEARS SHE IS NOT NECESSARY
Oh
Gertrude
Gertrude
Is
Whereas
Hamlet (*She shakes her head pitifully*)
Unnecessary Hamlet
IN THE DITCH WITH HIM
(*She goes to leave and stops*)
We planned your execution
It was in his diary
And not in pencil
Ink
The judges had been nominated and the trial was fixed
A contract with the axeman
Spanish
Far from cheap

(*She goes out. A stillness. Suddenly Albert declares himself*)

ALBERT: I'm not leaving (*Pause*)
I left before but I was young then (*Pause*)
A schoolboy (*Pause*)
Bundled on a train (*Pause*)
Books
Bags
Chucked after me
NEVER AGAIN (*He looks to Gertrude*)
I have an army on the frontier show me your arse
(*Gertrude looks mildly at Albert*)
You know armies (*He menaces her*)
How they love to march (*Pause*)
And burn
And crucify
(*She does not remove her eyes from him*)
Turn infants on their lances
Ravish
Trample
And halfway through some crime they cry I've
seen it in the East (*Pause*)
So show your arse (*Pause*)
Poor Denmark (*Pause*)
Show me it
(*Gertrude lifts her heavy black skirt, and poses for him. Albert passes a hand over his face in his ordeal. For a long time he contemplates the object of his passion*)

GERTRUDE: My unburied son
ALBERT: I'll bury him
(*A pause of inspiration*)
GERTRUDE: My unkilled lover
(*Albert hesitates. Gertrude gasps in an ecstasy. She lets fall her skirt and runs to Claudius, taking him in an adoring embrace and smothering him with kisses*)
CLAUDIUS: The cry
GERTRUDE: Yes
CLAUDIUS: Waiting
GERTRUDE: Yes
(*Claudius studies her*)

CLAUDIUS: Always I thought the cry was in you
But it's not
It's outside
It waits
It walks
Some long hound pacing the perimeter
Frost clinging to it
Clouds of breath
GERTRUDE: CALL IT
CALL IT
(*Claudius lingers, then tears away. Gertrude over-
comes her upheaval. With infinite calm, she
straightens her disordered clothes. Isola hurries
in, a white wedding garment over her arm*)

21

ISOLA: Cast your mind back (*She sniggers with pleasure*)
Cast your mind back and say who thought of it
(*Gertrude removes her black jacket*)
I DID
GERTRUDE: You did yes
ISOLA: That boy I said
That boy's a branch for you
(*Isola takes the jacket*)
NOT SUCH A BOY NOW
NO BOY THE DUKE OF
I *can* say it
MECKLENBURG
If you need to you can say a word previous to
this I never needed to
Duchess of MECKLENBURG
See
See
(*Gertrude steps out of her full black skirt*)
Gertrude I like you
I always did
We had our falling out but never could I bring
myself to
AND THAT WAS ALL CLAUDIUS

Howard Barker

THAT WAS MY BOY
I fretted
I thought you (*Pause. She takes the skirt*)
NEVER MIND WHAT I THOUGHT YOU
This is so discreet (*She holds up the white dress*)
At forty-three a bride should be
I say discreet
IS ISN'T THOUGH IS IT
(*She laughs and pretends to shake her head*)
NOT TERRIBLY
(*She laughs. Gertrude leaves her holding the garment*)

GERTRUDE: How delighted you are Isola
ISOLA: Delighted for you (*Pause*)
For you
(*In a moment of pity Gertrude draws Isola's face near to her own and kisses her*)
That's nice (*She almost sobs*)
That's nice of you
GERTRUDE: Not for me at all
Silly
Not for me
ISOLA: For Denmark obviously I don't know politics the way I used to do but Meckel (*She stops*)
Mickel (*She shakes her head*)
Can't say it Gertrude
GERTRUDE: Not Denmark
Nor Gertrude either
I ALSO AM MATERNAL AND I KNOW WHAT PLEASES YOU
(*Isola looks up at Gertrude*)
ISOLA: Give him an island
Far out in the Cold Sea
He'll plant
He might put up with me
Digging
A
Bit
(*Gertrude looks pityingly at Isola. She takes the garment and goes out with it*)
I HOPE YOU'RE HAPPY (*Pause*)
TWICE HIS AGE SO WHAT I'VE BEEN
(*Pause*)

Oh yes I've been (*Pause*)
In love with boys (*She reflects*)
(*Claudius enters*)
Forget her son forget her yes it can be done
forgetting impossible you say and then someone
it could be years it could be straightaway
(*Claudius goes to Isola and placing his hands
round her neck throttles her. Isola sinks to the
floor. Claudius lifts his hands free of her.
Gertrude enters in the wedding gown, glove-tight
on her*)

CLAUDIUS: The lies
The ludicrous lies
I cannot hear another lie however lovingly
intended you and I we never lied cruel it is the
place of never-lying look at us however were two
ever better made to thrive in such a landscape me
wire you stone I cannot look at you such
polished stone you are and the thin stuff drawn
over you your arse of stone your breasts of stone
and the thin stuff clinging (*He fights collapse*)
She would have
She
Ha
I PUT HER OUT HER MISERY ANOTHER
CHARITABLE ACT
To die at my hands
I don't see how she could object to that far better
surely than to see me
DIE AT YOURS
(*He shakes his head. Gertrude walks out*)
COME BACK
(*Something is flung in, and slides over the floor.
Claudius is still, sensing it, not seeing it. Pause*)
CASCAN
He's dead
CASCAN
Silly
Silly
CASCAN
DEAD OR NOT YOU LOOK
(*Pause and silence*)
I'll be Cascan

HIS BORROWED TONGUE
(*He mimics the manner of the servant*)
How well I understand from my somewhat
remote perspective
How often I observe the paradoxical
Characteristically the stratagems of those who
(*He crawls over the floor towards the flung bundle*)
And these manoeuvres whilst
(*He lifts a corner of the wrapping. He recognizes
the contents. He lets fall the wrapping. He turns,
still on his knees, hands at his sides, motionless*)
Ostensibly (*Pause*)
Antithesis (*Pause*)
Implicit (*Pause*)
Abstract
(*Ragusa walks in and instantly wails, covering her
face with her hands*)
Contradictory (*Pause*)
Delusion (*Pause*)
Implicated (*Pause. She howls on*)
Marginal
(*His list competes with Ragusa's despair*)
Dislocate
(*They compete*)
TRANSITIONAL (*Claudius covers his ears*)
TRANSITIONAL
ALL RIGHT
ALL RIGHT
(*She controls her wailing. Pause*)
Ragusa

RAGUSA: I have so
Oh
So envied you your
YOU MAY NOT LIVE OUTSIDE AS YOU
TWO DO YOU MAY NOT
(*Claudius is quite still*)
I held her under water
Easy
I HELD HER UNDER WATER NOT ALL
OF HER THE HEAD
Funny
When I came here I said
Funny

THE SHEER SAYING OF THESE PEOPLE
THE SHEER DOING OF THEM
(*She half-laughs*)
Admit it
I lie between you now
I divide your bed
(*Claudius does not move. Ragusa runs to him. She slaps him. She kisses him. She slaps him. She runs from the room. Claudius hangs his head*)

CLAUDIUS: Oh their poor crimes
(*He shakes his head. He retrieves the body of the child*)
The little mischiefs which they heap at the feet of God
(*He kisses her. Her places her tenderly in the arms of Isola*)
No wonder He smiles
(*The cathedral bells announce the wedding of Gertrude and Albert*)
Have you seen the smile of God
IT DRIPS COMPLACENCY AS A DOG'S JAW STREAMS SALIVA ON THE RUMOUR OF ITS FOOD
Gertrude
Gertrude
(*Gertrude walks in, hatted, suited, gloved for her honeymoon. At last the bells cease*)

GERTRUDE: Two weeks in a warm climate
Two weeks in a warm climate more is not possible the business of the government demands his swift return
Two weeks of too-red flowers
Two weeks of too-blue seas
And the villa secluded all nourishment brought to the room
How else should a woman learn her husband's ways
Which side of the bed he claims and if he lays an arm possessively across me shudders or is still
The scents at dusk
The casement creaking in warm airs
I'll sleep I'll sleep I'll sleep as simply as a child
And with his child inside me he declares we

cannot leave without an heir he sinks his mouth
into my hair and breathes me did you breathe me
there the odours of me I don't compare men men
compare already your acts are fainter than rinsed
drawings
WASH ME MY YOUNG HUSBAND WASH
ME SOAP THE DEAD MAN OFF MY SKIN
(*Pause. She recovers*)
And life with him
The making of a garden grey this garden every-
thing I plant grey we are northern are we not
great is the grey stone and the moss grey grey
waves and me grey naked I'll stoop even in frost
boots on my feet grey socks (*She seems to laugh*)
And he shaving in a so-high window will glance
from the mirror to my arse
Grey garden
Grey garden
Ashes scattered on it
Scattered ashes of burned men
HE'LL RUSH TO FUCK
HE'LL RUSH TO FUCK
AND OUR SLIDING HEELS WILL TREAD
YOU IN
(*Pause. She looks at the still form of Claudius,
kneeling*)
Why don't you
Why don't you
(*Gertrude slips off the chair and goes to him, to
take his head in her hands. as she does so, her
great cry comes, not from herself, but from the
land. She is seized by it. Claudius is dead and she
struggles with the weight of his body. As she sup-
ports it against her hips, Albert enters, in a travel-
ling coat, and observes the spectacle....*)

ALBERT: Come now
(*Gertrude emits a sob, a shudder. Claudius slips to
her feet*)
Come now
(*Gertrude, sensing her condition, reaches into her
pocket for a small bag and removes a lipstick and
powder from it, and holds up a mirror*)
Stay like that

GERTRUDE: But I'm
ALBERT: Like that
(*She turns a ruined face to him*)
Adored like that
(*She concedes. She walks smartly to the door. He follows. He turns to call an order*)
BURN THESE
BURN AND SCATTER THESE
(*They go*)

KNOWLEDGE AND A GIRL

(*The Snow White Case*)

Snow White's wicked step-mother was also bidden to the feast. But iron slippers had already been put upon the fire, and they were brought in with tongs, and set before her. Then she was forced to put on the red-hot shoes, and dance until she dropped down dead.

The Brothers Grimm
'Little Snow White'

CHARACTERS

Queen	Of a Great Place
King	Of a Great Place
Snow White	Daughter of the King
Servant	A Forester
Jane	A Maid to the Queen
Sara	A Maid to the Queen
Askew	King of All the Irish
Old Woman	A Mirror to the Queen
Young Askew	Prince of All the Irish
Smith	An Iron worker

SCENE 1

A Queen naked in a forest.

QUEEN: Infantile he calls me
Is that not a lovely word?
He thinks the word humiliates me but I like the word
I wear the word
I walk in it
You say it
You say infantile
SERVANT: Infantile
QUEEN: Now slap me
Slap the woman who is infantile
(*The servant slaps*)
YOU HAVE SLAPPED A QUEEN SLAPPED A QUEEN AND STRIPPED HER GOD HELP YOU WHEN I TELL
SERVANT: (*Aghast*) Tell?
QUEEN: Tell yes
Have I not a husband?
Is my husband not the king?
SERVANT: The king yes
QUEEN: And kings must know
They must know everything
DON'T SQUIRM
DON'T TWIST AWAY LIKE THAT
OH SILLY WOODMAN
Your fluid trickles down my thigh your stuff is in my womb or higher higher than my womb and hot such hot stuff yours
Give me my pants now give me my bra or do you want them
YOU WANT THEM BUT YOU'RE IN SUCH A TERROR THEY'LL BE DISCOVERED IN YOUR ROOM
The King would cut your head off
With your own axe

The woodman chopped
That would amuse him
And me
It would amuse me too
If you are afraid to take my underwear then steal my shoes

SERVANT: Your shoes
But what's the queen without her shoes

QUEEN: I don't know what am I without my shoes
A child perhaps
Swim me
Swim me who is nothing without shoes

SERVANT: I'll swim you
I'll shudder you and turn your darkness inside out
I'll make you scream with labour

QUEEN: Yes

SERVANT: I'll see you stagger under infants that hang off your breasts

QUEEN: Do
Do

SERVANT: RINSE
FLOOD
AND WRECK YOUR TAUT QUEEN'S BELLY YOU (*The Queen laughs*)

QUEEN: Taut yes
So taut and never stretched my belly
If any man can stretch me that man's you

SCENE 2

The corridor of a palace

SNOW WHITE: The King of All the Irish wants to eat my mother

KING: Eat her?

SNOW WHITE: (*giggling*) Eat her yes
His eyes are knives and forks

KING: It's you that should be eaten

SNOW WHITE: It's me yes
After all I am fresh whereas the queen my mother has been eaten oh so many times

	Her arse has bites in it
KING:	Is that so?
SNOW WHITE:	Oh yes
	I must not be beastly and her breasts have all these little
	I must not be beastly
	Little lines and creases
	Tucks
	And
	Pleats
KING:	As if someone took a pencil
SNOW WHITE:	A pencil yes and scratched them very deeply
KING:	Yes and yet
SNOW WHITE:	Exactly
	YES AND YET (*She laughs*)
	Dear daddy come and see my garden
KING:	I have seen your garden
SNOW WHITE:	Not today
KING:	Today I have not seen it but we have a guest
	Show the Irish king your garden
SNOW WHITE:	That would be civil
KING:	Very civil yes and it would spare the Queen perhaps from being eaten
SNOW WHITE:	Yes (*She claps her hands with delight*)
QUEEN:	This Irishman
KING:	Yes
QUEEN:	Has offered me a child
KING:	Is that so?
QUEEN:	Obliquely
KING:	Obliquely obviously
QUEEN:	Late Summer he says
	I liked this
	Is a fruitful time
KING:	Poetic are the Irish and his room is number
QUEEN:	I know the number
KING:	Number nine
QUEEN:	Nine yes he carved it in the tablecloth
KING:	Exquisite manners
	Uttering the details of a rendezvous is sordid is it not
QUEEN:	I'll go if it amuses you
KING:	Amuses me?

QUEEN:	Since I can't provide him with a child my first service to my lord must be to entertain him and what's more entertaining than the spectacle of ambitious men thinking to succeed where he knows full well they can only fail? Let them hang off the cliff of my sterility like climbers absurdly kicking on their ropes no foothold nothing sheer and barren walled my womb (*Pause*)
KING:	You are utterly beautiful
QUEEN:	Yes
KING:	Beautiful And A Rage To Me
SNOW WHITE:	(*Returning*) My real mother
QUEEN:	Yes
SNOW WHITE:	She wore loose gowns
QUEEN:	Is that so?
SNOW WHITE:	Oh yes most certainly but of thin stuff which when the wind blew clung I say wind even breezes or simply moving could do it apparently I shall wear thin gowns Your clothing whereas it strives to be provocative is possibly I MUST NOT BE UNKIND
QUEEN:	Oh do Do be unkind if that's what you need to be
SNOW WHITE:	(*Puzzled*) Need to be? Can one need unkindness? (*Pause*)
QUEEN:	Oh yes one can (*Pause*)
SNOW WHITE:	Very well You advertize your body with these tight garments when really you are rather old (*Pause*)
KING:	What did he think of the garden our Irish king? They can't grow Chinese herbs as you do but not everybody likes them Chinese herbs and pink is not to everybody's liking either (*Pause*)

SNOW WHITE: Forgive me
                    Your body is excellently formed and
                    Men find you so
                    I have finished with my garden
                    I am not a child
                    It is a child's garden silly pink and (*She hurries
                    away in a rush of tears*)

SCENE 3

A mirror breaking.

SARA: God
            Oh
            God (*Pause*)
QUEEN: You are doing this deliberately
SARA: I am not Madam God's my judge but it must
            seem so it slipped out my fingers
QUEEN: It did slip out your fingers but you intended
            that it should
SARA: I cannot contradict you Madam but if I
            do intend to break these mirrors I do not
            know I do and I am most awfully sorry to
            intend it
QUEEN: Three now
SARA: Three yes
QUEEN: Have slipped out of your fingers
SARA: I am not fit to be the Queen's maid nor any-
            body else's I am clumsy ugly and I have
            betrayed your confidence please replace me
            Jane is such a sweet girl give Jane my post
            she never drops things Jane at least so far as
            I know I tell a lie she dropped a jug once I'll
            fetch a broom (*Pause*) Shall I? (*Pause*)
QUEEN: No the dropping of these mirrors cannot be
            coincidence but if we choose to believe your
            protestations that ill-will forms no part of it we
            must conclude either that you are suffering a
            sickness or (*Pause*)
            This is more difficult but I must be logical
            (*Pause*)
            I am not meant to see my face (*Pause*)

	Ask Jane up with a mirror if she can discover one
SARA:	I AM SO VERY VERY SORRY
QUEEN:	Shh
SARA:	SO SORRY MADAM
QUEEN:	I know you are
SARA:	You have been so perfectly kind to me
QUEEN:	I have not I have not been kind to you at all
SARA:	YOU HAVE
QUEEN:	All right

QUEEN: Sometimes
Sometimes I have
Get the broom now get the broom and Jane
(*The servant's footsteps crunch on glass*)

KING: Did you go to Number nine?

QUEEN: Nine? (*Pause*)
No I didn't go to Number nine

JANE: Mirror Madam

QUEEN: Mirror yes
(*A broom sweeps broken glass*)
DON'T PROP IT HOLD IT
Tilt it
This way
To the light
The light

KING: You didn't go to Number nine?

QUEEN: More
More tilt than that
Thank you
Now at last a queen is able to observe herself she is not
obliged to go into the courtyard and stare into pools
it's a miracle I say observe I think I must mean contemplate

KING: He says you did

QUEEN: Contemplate the shape of pain

JANE: Pain? But Madam is so beautiful today

QUEEN: Shh

JANE: She is beautiful every day but

QUEEN: Shh
Shh
Silly Jane
The pain's not mine
But his

JANE: His?

QUEEN:	His whoever beholds me
KING:	What makes me inclined to believe him
	(*The sound of a breaking mirror*)
JANE:	Oh
	Oh
	Oh
KING:	Is the fact that he has submitted a request to stay
JANE:	I NEVER NEVER DROP THINGS
KING:	A few weeks longer
	Weeks note
	Not days
QUEEN:	The hunting?
KING:	Ah
	The hunting
	I never thought about the hunting
	Does he hunt?
QUEEN:	How would I know?
KING:	I've not seen him hunting
JANE:	Beat me
	Beat me
QUEEN:	Yes
	I expect I will
JANE:	BEAT ME PLEASE
QUEEN:	It isn't hunting then
	(*She walks. The crunch of shattered glass*)
	The mirrors are against me
	Or the servants
	Possibly they are
JANE:	No
	Madam
	No
QUEEN:	It is cheaper to replace the servants than the mirrors
JANE:	(*Distraut*) Don't replace the servants Ma'am
QUEEN:	The mirrors come from Venice whereas you where are you from?
JANE:	Down the lane Ma'am
QUEEN:	Down the lane
	And down that filthy lane there are a hundred girls as clumsy and illiterate as you
JANE:	OH BEAT ME MA'AM
QUEEN:	You are dismissed
JANE:	BEAT ME
	(*Pause. Jane recovers*)

Madam
I have a sick child and a mother who is legless
blind and 92 (*Pause*)

QUEEN: Dismissed I said
(*Jane goes to leave*)
This mother
Can she hold a mirror still? (*Pause*)

JANE: Yes I
YES YES HER WRISTS ARE QUITE

QUEEN: Fetch her

KING: If it isn't hunting keeps him here it must be you
And you
Even if you have not submitted to him yet
He obviously expects you to

QUEEN: That would explain his reluctance to depart

KING: It would yes
I HATE THE WAY HE LOOKS AT
YOU

QUEEN: Get rid of him

KING: STARING AND

QUEEN: Tell him pack his bags

KING: FINGERS ALL

QUEEN: His people upset ours

KING: THE WAY HE PUTS HIS FINGERS IN
HIS MOUTH
HAVE YOU SEEN IT

QUEEN: Grabbing them in corridors and so on

KING: HAVE YOU I SAID

QUEEN: I've seen it yes
He stares at me and puts his fingers in his
mouth
I stare back
Let him suffer
Let him squirm for me
The stare's contempt

KING: Is it
Is it contempt
I never know with you

QUEEN: How good that is
How good you never know with me

SCENE 4

Snow White naked in the forest

SNOW WHITE: I've seen you with my mother
I've seen you and it's death if I should tell
I say death
OH WHAT A WHAT A DEATH (*She laughs*)
They burned a traitor yesterday and upside down why upside down no reason apparently and then a horse trod on him a big horse a cart horse and it was specially trained yes trained to tread on people whilst being unafraid of flames now that is unusual because horses hate fire (*Pause*)
The death that traitor got whilst spectacularly horrid would represent only a fraction of the imagination my father would invest in devising a suitable punishment for you and he only sold some papers that traitor WHEREAS YOU (*She laughs*)
QUEEN THIEF
The Queen my Mother's legs are long but mine are longer
White and long
Exquisite my legs are
The King of All the Irish said so
What you do with the Queen my Mother do with me
The same
The same exactly (*Pause*)
SERVANT: The same is difficult
SNOW WHITE: Difficult why?
SERVANT: I'm not the same myself
SNOW WHITE: Try
SERVANT: Try
(*Patiently*) A man is what he is because a woman makes him if you change the woman then the man's changed you're not your mother you're your mother's daughter now it may be your mother's daughter could have a powerful effect on me and the King of All the Irish has

good judgement about your legs their length their whiteness and so on I agree so something might occur but not the same not nearly the same I think let alone the same exactly (*Pause*)
Miss (*Pause*)

SNOW WHITE: I'm not a child

SERVANT: No

SNOW WHITE: It is the Queen my Mother who is infantile not me

SERVANT: Yes

SNOW WHITE: And whereas she might benefit from your elucidations I require nothing but your acquiescence in what I have proposed to you
If I do not know everything I shall do

SERVANT: Yes

SNOW WHITE: Consider yourself an element of my education

SERVANT: I will do

(*Snow White laughs*)

SNOW WHITE: I've told you off and now you won't want to kiss
Say you like me (*Pause*)
I am more beautiful than the Queen my Mother her breasts are gnawn her breasts have tucks and pleats and she has never fed a baby (*Pause*)
Say you like me

SCENE 5

Mischievous behaviour in a corridor. Fading laughter.

OLD WOMAN: You could always hang the mirror lady
You could hang it on a nail that's what most people do

QUEEN: I like it held

OLD WOMAN: You like it held that's up to you you are the queen and what you like is good enough for me the nail's put many out of work who could have stood and held things certainly

QUEEN: You talk too much

OLD WOMAN: Do I beg pardon

QUEEN: On the other hand you don't drop things apparently

OLD WOMAN:	I hang on like grim death
QUEEN:	Good
OLD WOMAN:	It comes of being blind
	You drop a thing
	You end up crawling on your hands and knees
QUEEN:	You're blind and yet you tilt the glass precisely
	Are you sure you can't see me?
OLD WOMAN:	I'm sure lady
	(*Brouhaha in the corridor*)
	Your hair's longer
QUEEN:	I'm growing it
OLD WOMAN:	Growing it that's unusual if you'll excuse me the older woman generally has short hair but she can pin it up (*Pause*)
	I couldn't stick that noise if it was me lived here
QUEEN:	His retinue is boisterous but the King of All the Irish he is quiet (*Pause*)
	Thoughtful (*Pause*)
	And looks a great deal preferring looks to speech (*Pause*)
	These looks like summer rain fall on my neck warm rain my neck which is not young my hips my thighs still firm my thighs thin skinned my thighs however and blue veined
OLD WOMAN:	Lady
	The sound of your heels paints your body on my blindness even
	Your walk's a legend
	Five steps and his mouth went dry
KING:	(*Hurtling in*) I'VE BEEN STRUCK
	OH LISTEN I'VE BEEN STRUCK
QUEEN:	Struck
	Who struck you?
KING:	Here
	Here
QUEEN:	Where?
KING:	THE CHEEK THE CHEEK
QUEEN:	Yes
	Oh
	Yes
	Oh
	Darling
KING:	IN MY OWN PLACE

QUEEN:	Yes
KING:	PREPOSTEROUS
OLD WOMAN:	Poor king I was only saying my own lane's a pigsty but a quiet one compared to this
QUEEN:	This is not a pigsty
OLD WOMAN:	No but pigs run round in it
KING:	They must go home
QUEEN:	Yes
KING:	Now
QUEEN:	Yes the retinue must be reduced
KING:	NOT REDUCED DISMISSED AND HIM TOO
QUEEN:	Him?
KING:	THE KING OF ALL THE IRISH
OLD WOMAN:	He's not the trouble though is he he only looks
KING:	Who is this vile old woman?
OLD WOMAN:	Vile
QUEEN:	She holds the mirror
OLD WOMAN:	Vile but better than a nail apparently
KING:	Kiss
	Kiss the place
	(*The Queen kisses him*)
	The idiot who struck me thought I was some- one else
	Too bad for him
	The hand that did it
	BURNED BEFORE HIS EYES
QUEEN:	Shh
KING:	Kiss
	Kiss (*He laughs low*)
	No not burned
	A DOG WILL EAT IT A STARVED DOG
QUEEN:	Yes
	Yes
KING:	MY OWN DOG POSSIBLY
QUEEN:	Yes
KING:	LET MY OWN DOG CRUNCH HIS BONES
	(*He catches his breath*)
	Oh God your thighs
QUEEN:	Shh
KING:	A flood is
QUEEN:	Shh I said

KING:	Travelling down your thighs
QUEEN:	(*Urgently*) SHE'S BLIND SHE IS NOT DEAF
	Catch me
	Turn me to the glass
	Let me watch your agony
	OH AM I KILLING YOU
	(*Her clothing is violently disturbed*)
	OH SAY MY BEAUTY IS YOUR DEATH
	(*A gasp. A pause*)
OLD WOMAN:	Quiet now the Irish
	They've learned their lesson possibly
	It takes a blow
	Oh yes
	It takes that fractional excess
	(*A little cry from the Queen*)
	To bring us back to moderation
	Do you need the mirror lady?
	Can I go?

SCENE 6

In room 9.

ASKEW:	Your life's empty
QUEEN:	Is it?
ASKEW:	I know queens who do good work
	I know queens who get their hands dirty
QUEEN:	These dirty queens
	You can't sleep for thinking of them naked I suppose?
ASKEW:	They visit slums
	They pick up babies
QUEEN:	These queens who smell of piss and milk
	You steal their underwear
ASKEW:	YOU'RE TOO CLEVER YOU'RE TOO SARCASTIC I WOULD SLAP YOU IF YOU WERE MY BITCH AND SO SHOULD HE YOUR HUSBAND (*Pause*)
QUEEN:	(*Amused*) I irritate you
ASKEW:	I'm not irritated I'm giving you advice
	Queens have functions
	Queens have tasks

QUEEN: (*Violently*) DON'T REMIND ME OF THE
TASKS OF QUEENS
THEY HAVE A SINGLE TASK
THE TASK IS BIRTH (*Pause*)

ASKEW: I must go home
I've hung about here pretending to admire
views

QUEEN: You have

ASKEW: Planting ceremonial trees

QUEEN: You have hung about
You have planted a lot of trees

ASKEW: When everybody knows I

QUEEN: It's on the walls (*Pause*)

ASKEW: What is?

QUEEN: The thing that everybody knows (*Pause*)
We wash it off we scrape it off not we the
workmen wash it off and come the morning
there it is again (*Pause*)
This ugly phrase (*Pause*)
Ugly
But
True (*Pause*)

ASKEW: Say it

QUEEN: Can't

ASKEW: Can't say it?

QUEEN: I don't say these words

ASKEW: You do you do say them I never knew a
woman used more words worse words the
words that come cascading out of you when
you

QUEEN: SOMETIMES
SOMETIMES I DO (*Pause*)
Very well (*Pause*)
The Queen's gob's full of Irish (*She stops*)
I can't say it
I can't say the word (*Pause*)
You must be going

ASKEW: Yes
Yes I (*A swift move*)
IT ISN'T HEALTHY HERE

QUEEN: No
The rooms are damp

ASKEW: (*Turning on her*) NOT THE ROOMS THE PEOPLE NOT THE DAMP THE (*Pause*)
I hesitate to use the word I am a guest

QUEEN: Outrageous guest

ASKEW: (*Stung*) Indecent hosts (*Pause*)
Forgive me
Forgive me

QUEEN: Yes
Your manners by and large have been impeccable

ASKEW: (*Suddenly enraged again*) AND YOU HAVE A DAUGHTER THE PAIR OF YOU

QUEEN: Yes

ASKEW: A SWEET AND (*Pause*)
The word's depravity

SCENE 7

SNOW WHITE: The King of All the Irish has a son
The Prince of All the Irish
And when he left he said to me
Squeezing my hand

QUEEN: He does squeeze hands

SNOW WHITE: He does
He is forever squeezing hands
He said to me
This son would visit
And
And
This is funny
RESCUE ME (*A weak laugh*)

QUEEN: Rescue indeed
FROM WHOM?

SNOW WHITE: That's what I said (*They laugh*)
And he said you
THE DEPRAVITY
His favourite word
OF THE QUEEN YOUR MOTHER
The depravity (*Pause*)
I looked it up
This word

And I thought it could equally apply to me
I look at you
I see the lines around your mouth
Your cruel mouth
Chiselled deeper every day
And your hands
STAINED BY FORNICATION
Yes
Oh yes
THE RACE OF YOUR DECAY
And you'd think there's cause for satisfaction
Rejoice
Snow White whose excellence is blinding
Yes
As snow is blinding
I have seen men turn their eyes away (*She
laughs*)
I'm frightened I am not desirable (*A silence*)
I said

QUEEN: Yes (*Pause*)
SNOW WHITE: You wish to annihilate me
I confess my deepest and most
I STRIP OUT MY HORROR AND SHOW
IT LIKE A VEIN TO YOU AND YOU
You
Do not extend one hand to comfort me
If I were a dog you'd settle my head in your
skirt animal gaze to woman's gaze some kind-
ness would flow
OH LET ME BE A DOG
(*Pause. A swift recovery*)
I want to leave
I want to leave
I am fascinated by you
I want to leave (*Pause*)
DO NOT SEEK ME (*Pause*)

QUEEN: Of course I shall not seek you (*Pause*)
SNOW WHITE: I could have so loved you
QUEEN: I know
But to have been loved by you I should have
had to cease being myself

SCENE 8

The servant and the King in the forest.

SERVANT: She lives with men
KING: What kind of men?
SERVANT: Strangers
KING: Show me the strangers
SERVANT: I can't
KING: Why can't you?
SERVANT: I can't discover them
KING: (*Chagrined*) You are a forester
SERVANT: I am Head of all your foresters but whole miles
            of this have never yet been trodden
KING: TREAD IT NOW (*The servant scoffs*)
            DON'T SCOFF
            DON'T SNORT
SERVANT: Your Majesty must know it is too big the
            forest (*Pause*)
KING: Yes
            And how proud I was that men could disappear
            in it
            Drown in its pools
            Or limp back raving from the torture of its
            insects
            Such density of oak I said
            To foreign dignitaries
            No man ever possessed (*Pause*)
            And now these same oaks conceal my daughter
            My daughter and the strangers who at this very
            moment possibly
            HANG HER BY HER HEELS FROM
            THOSE GREAT BRANCHES
SERVANT: Oh I don't think
KING: STRIP HER THRASH HER AND
SERVANT: I don't think so
KING: HOW DO YOU KNOW
            YOU KNOW NOTHING OF THE FOREST
            (*Pause*)
            I apologize
            You know a great deal of the forest
            But rather little of these strangers I suggest
            (*Pause*)

	Pin up notices
	Say I pine
	Say I beg for her
SERVANT:	Yes
KING:	Scour in so far as scouring can be done and if you stumble on them be conciliatory no matter how offensive ugly cruel or what they are DO NOT ANTAGONIZE THESE STRANGERS THEY MAY KILL (*Pause*)
	Later
	I will invent a death for them
SERVANT:	The King is as famous for the variety of his executions as for the breadth of his forests or (*Pause*)
	If I may say so (*Pause*)
	The beauty of his wife (*Pause*)
KING:	The Queen is beautiful is she?
	According to you?
SERVANT:	I rarely see the Queen but on the few occasions I
KING:	She's 41 (*Pause*)
SERVANT:	41 is she? (*He falters*)
	Her beauty is undiminished no matter what her
KING:	Undiminished is it?
	According to you? (*Pause*)
	What does a forester know of undiminished beauty?
	It's trees he knows about
	Trees
	Presumably? (*Pause*)
	Undiminished

SCENE 9

The old woman holds the mirror.

KING:	Undiminished says the coarse axeman
	But it isn't true
	It is diminished
	Or possibly he studies you more closely than I do

QUEEN: No one studies me more closely than you
                do

KING: Possibly this hard knuckled connoisseur of
                trees finds in your thigh the power and the
                polish of the yew

QUEEN: Possibly

KING: The beech
                The ash
                Stripped of their barks these woods are pale
                and sinewy I think of your limbs as willow
                personally

QUEEN: I know nothing of trees

KING: Warm willow

QUEEN: I can't distinguish one tree from another

KING: Does he say willow? Or is it only me says
                willow? (*Pause*)

OLD WOMAN: A man carved me (*Pause*)
                Talking of woods and women (*Pause*)
                Carved me with initials (*Pause*)
                There he said
                You're property (*she laughs*)
                The thigh that was (*Pause*)
                I expect you'd like to see

KING: DO NOT EXPOSE YOUR FLESH YOU
                ARE FULLY CLOTHED EVEN OFF-
                ENSIVE TO ME

QUEEN: Show
                Show

KING: DRAW DOWN HER FILTHY SKIRT

QUEEN: I want to see
                (*The old woman hoists her skirt. Pause. The
                Queen laughs a little, sweetly*)
                Ridiculous the relics of desire

OLD WOMAN: That was my first husband
                The second
                Oh didn't he rant on
                It's permanent I said
                So he flings me over
                Arse upper

KING: THAT I DO NOT WISH TO SEE

OLD WOMAN: AND CARVES THAT (*She cackles*)

QUEEN: Put down the mirror now
                You may go

OLD WOMAN:	Madam
	Forgive me
	An old woman should never show above the knee
	(*The old woman withdraws. Pause*)
QUEEN:	I love you but (*Pause. She breathes irregularly*)
	I love you but
KING:	It's all right
	To
	Love
	Me
	But
	Is
	All
	Right
	With
	Me
	(*The Queen sobs*)

SCENE 10

A flock of pigeons rises.

YOUNG ASKEW:	It took no time at all
SNOW WHITE:	What didn't
YOUNG ASKEW:	To find you
SNOW WHITE:	Pity
YOUNG ASKEW:	I set out with a premise
	Which is not I hasten to add a conviction
	Says all men are liars
SNOW WHITE:	I'm a liar
YOUNG ASKEW:	There you are
	This premise has much to recommend it obviously
SNOW WHITE:	I don't like you
YOUNG ASKEW:	By taking it as axiomatic that all directions I received were mischievous I expended only a fraction of the energy that might have been consumed if I had followed these directions to the letter

SNOW WHITE: I don't like you at all
YOUNG ASKEW: On the other hand I was careful not to replace one prejudice by another
I did not for example simply substitute a right-hand turning for a left (*Pause*)
I intend to marry you so whether you like me or not is neither here nor there (*Pause*)
My father was correct you have skin of perfect whiteness but do you wash at all (*He laughs*)
SNOW WHITE: I live with seven men
YOUNG ASKEW: Is that so?
And does that make you disinclined to wash?
SNOW WHITE: It does (*Pause*)
YOUNG ASKEW: Come here
I'll wash you
I'll wash you myself
SNOW WHITE: GET AWAY I'LL CALL THE SEVEN MEN (*Pause*)
YOUNG ASKEW: You see the horse there?
It is mine
Get on it
Do not collect your clothes
You are very beautiful and this beauty whilst you may think it offers you the key to many things is in fact a gaol I will help you I will free you from the gaol of your own beauty
On the horse now
On the horse I said
SNOW WHITE: I SLEEP WITH SEVEN MEN (*Pause*)
YOUNG ASKEW: The seven men I'll wash away (*Pause*)
SNOW WHITE: Yes (*Pause*)
And it's not nice here
Pretty
Pretty certainly but when it rains oh the dismal music of the pool
AND DAMP (*She laughs*)
You open a drawer and there's a toad
Yes
SQUATTING IN YOUR UNDERWEAR

(*Pause*)
I have no underwear I lost it months ago
I live here naked which they prefer it saves
them the trouble of undressing me if you
like me steal me

SCENE 11

Euphoric running on a stone staircase. Ecstatic male laughter.

KING:	THE PRINCE OF ALL THE IRISH
	HAS
	SAVED
	MY
	LIFE
	SAVED SNOW WHITE
	SNOW WHITE AND HER DOTING PARENT TOO
JANE:	(*Amused*) The King is like a boy today
QUEEN:	Yes
	But he is not a boy king is he?
	I'll wear the white thing
JANE:	Madam must allow a father to express his joy in whatever way he
QUEEN:	Must I
	Are you telling me what I must allow get the white dress down the one with all the buttons and never tell me what I must allow the buttons from the ankle to the neck
	I am enclosed today I am a sheath of bruise and tenderness no a man should not be a boy for all that boys are beautiful their beauty stops

SCENE 12

A room of torture. A cry.

KING:	(*Walking pensively*) The seven strangers did not know Snow White
	(*A cry*)

They are unanimous they had never even
heard of her and in their innocence assumed
all women here had skin like hers
(*A cry*)
I'm blinding them since they make such bad
use of their eyes
(*A cry*)
And let them trespass with their hands stuck
out
Sprawling over tree roots
Plunging into pools
When winter's gone I'll hound what's
left

YOUNG ASKEW: Yes (*Pause*)
Yes I
KING: Oh don't be critical
YOUNG ASKEW: With all respect
I
KING: Don't I said
YOUNG ASKEW: Cannot for my own part overlook the fact
of Snow White's own admission that she
wholeheartedly
KING: I like you very much
And your face
I do think you have such a strong and pen-
sive face
NO WONDER SNOW WHITE LOVES
YOU
JUSTICE DOES NOT INTEREST ME
IT'S MY OFFENCE (*Pause*)
With all respect
(*A cry*)
That's being rinsed out here
(*A cry*)
YES
AND I CAN WATCH I DO NOT CREEP
AWAY TO PICNIC
Some monarchs do
They hurry off with hampers and women in
thin skirts
Lying on their backs they watch the sky
through trees
While who they hurtled to oblivion shrieks

and dies
I take it as the burden of my office to see my
instinct through
Do look me in the eyes
You will be my son soon and my heir
And now I'm going to the chapel to offer up
a prayer not for these blind men but for
you
I have a horror you are an idealist

SCENE 13

The old woman with the mirror and the Queen.

QUEEN:	I'm pregnant
	(*Pause. Distant drilling of soldiers*)
	I said I'm
OLD WOMAN:	Madam (*Pause*)
QUEEN:	I was so sick this morning
	Like an animal I
OLD WOMAN:	I heard
QUEEN:	Like an animal in a stall this
OLD WOMAN:	Yes
QUEEN:	Noise
	Coming from me (*Pause*)
	I AM 41 (*Pause*)
OLD WOMAN:	But so young Lady so tight on the bones
QUEEN:	IN TWO MONTHS IT WILL SHOW
	(*Pause*)
OLD WOMAN:	I think my lady must accept some alteration
	in her shape is going to occur if not sooner
	then later but this may not offend her hus-
	band in my experience men find
QUEEN:	IT WILL OFFEND HIM
OLD WOMAN:	Some pleasure in the belly of a wife who
QUEEN:	PLEASURE IF THE CHILD IS HIS
OLD WOMAN:	Might I be so bold as to suggest
	If you have not in recent days
	You swiftly go to bed with him
QUEEN:	I have been
	In recent days
	In distant days

	For twenty years of days to bed with him (*Pause*)
OLD WOMAN:	Then where have you been lady? (*Pause*)
QUEEN:	My womb's tripped me
	Pretending all these years to be a desert at this least perfect of all moments it goes lush
	My desert is a river suddenly
	AND MY STERILITY HAS BEEN THE LEGEND OF THIS PLACE (*Pause*)
	I'm glad
	I'm glad of course
	Aren't I?
	Glad
	Obviously
	Glad
	Of course
OLD WOMAN:	Oh lady
	You pregnant and your daughter marrying
	Your daughter seventeen and you
	Oh lady where have you been?

SCENE 14

A seascape.

QUEEN:	I'm glad
	I'm glad of course
	Glad obviously
YOUNG ASKEW:	Yes
	Your husband has an heir but
QUEEN:	BY HIS OWN HEIR
	YOUR EYES DON'T CLING TO ME
	Why don't they cling
YOUNG ASKEW:	They do
QUEEN:	They cling and then they slip
YOUNG ASKEW:	I cannot be forever staring at a thing no matter how the thing
QUEEN:	Why not
	WHY NOT STARE UNTIL YOUR EYES TURN RED
	What would your eyes prefer to gaze on sand there's sand how dull how utterly

repetitive sand is seagulls there are seagulls
they weave the same old knots
I'M NEVER THE SAME
MY BREASTS ARE ALTERING
AND THIS SWELLING BETWEEN MY HIPS
I AGE AND YET I'M FERTILE

YOUNG ASKEW: I came here
Oh so like the young prince the young prince proverbial
And like the young prince boiling with contempt for my father his presence made my hair rise and he let me know he slept with you he did not say he could not say the words he let me know by winks your husband had been cuckolded
I DID FIND THAT LOATHSOME
So swore to be the perfect guest here and a servant to your husband and seeing Snow White (*Pause*)
Claimed her (*Pause*)
And then saw you (*Pause*)
Or more precisely heard you
The compelling rhythm of your heels on stone
HOW LITTLE DID I WANT TO BE WHERE HIM THE KING OF ALL THE IRISH HAD

QUEEN: I did not encourage you

YOUNG ASKEW: No
I was not encouraged and this lack of encouragement (*Pause*)
Encouraged me
IN YOUR BELLY I DEFEATED HIM
I am confessing to your husband

QUEEN: Silly

YOUNG ASKEW: Say it was the

QUEEN: Silly

YOUNG ASKEW: SAY THE CIRCUMSTANCES MADE OUR INTIMACY A FORGONE CONCLUSION
I'LL MARCH INTO HIS ROOM
NO KNOCKING

THREE UNFALTERING STRIDES
THE DOOR STILL WHINING ON ITS
HINGE
I LOVE YOUR WIFE (*Pause*)
Terrible utterance (*Pause*)
And then the terrible corollary
YOUR WIFE LOVES ME (*Pause*)

QUEEN: I don't love you
(*The sea*)

YOUNG ASKEW: Ah (*Pause*)
That vastly diminishes the attraction of my sacrifice
(*Pause. The sea breaks*)
The case is altered obviously (*Pause*)
A Prince is strangely suspended between his function and his appetite on the one hand he experiences the strict but not unsatisfying bondage of a code whose terms are unnegotiable but on the other he keeps as it were in play the prospect of its violation so
(*Askew's voice fades as the Queen walks on the soft sand*)

QUEEN: How lonely
How unexpected the loneliness of pregnancy
(*the sea*)
I DON'T FEEL GOOD IN THIS CHILD'S COMPANY

SNOW WHITE: (*Amused*) Is that the Prince?

QUEEN: He talks to himself

SNOW WHITE: Yes

QUEEN: And waves his arms about

SNOW WHITE: Yes

QUEEN: It's unnecessary and diminishes his authority
(*The sea*)

SNOW WHITE: You look nothing without heels (*Pause*)
All my life I have been frightened of you but really I was frightened of your heels
(*They laugh*)
I SHOULD HAVE MET YOU ON THE BEACH MORE OFTEN

QUEEN: I was never on the beach

SNOW WHITE: (*Darkly*) You were in the forest
QUEEN: Yes
               But pregnant women we are seized from the
               inside
               Abducted by our progeny
               MORE SUGAR MORE SALT
               NOW A WALK BY THE SEA
               He says the tenant of my belly (*Pause*)
               I daresay it's he
               (*The sea*)
SNOW WHITE: Pregnant?
               You?
QUEEN: Yes
SNOW WHITE: IF THERE'S TO BE A PREGNANCY (*She
               gasps*)
QUEEN: It should be yours?
SNOW WHITE: I SLEPT WITH SEVEN MEN
               (*The sea*)
               These footprints in the sand
               Go round and round
               The footprints of the Queen my mother and
               the Irish Prince
               Round and round as if
               The dance of anguished conversationalists
               I never knew you even spoke
               (*The sea*)

SCENE 15

A workshop. The hammering of iron.

KING: These shoes
               (*he half-laughs*)
               I pinched them from the Queen's wardrobe
               Yes
               And felt a schoolboy's luscious guilt
               Look at the label
SMITH: Crig – non
KING: Crignon yes
               All her garments come from France
               Now copy Monsieur Crignon
SMITH: (*Puzzled*) Copy?

KING:	Yes
	In iron
	DON'T SMILE
	It is an act of piety to create a shoe like this
	DON'T SMILE I SAID
	Shoes also are an act of faith
	Shoes also are devotions
	Study the heel
	Which lifts her perfect leg
	Which tilts her perfect hip
	The accomplice to men's agony Monsieur Crignon is
	THAT SMILE IS CRITICAL OF ME
	SINCE I MARRIED HER I'VE KNOWN NO PEACE (*Pause*)
SMITH:	Sir
KING:	When peace surely is the function of a marriage?
	When marriage is the truce?
SMITH:	Sir
KING:	Oh yes
	The thriving estates of marriages
	The planting
	The harvesting
	And great barns stacked with mutual love
	I DON'T KNOW WHY I TALK TO YOU
	WHO ARE YOU ANYWAY
SMITH:	No one sir
	(*Hammering of iron*)
KING:	Just make the shoes and keep your criticism to yourself
SMITH:	I have no criticism sir
KING:	Really?
	No criticism?
	That is nice of you
	That's very nice
	(*Hammering*)
	I've crushed the shoes
	My darling's shoes
	Oh dear
	Oh my dear's shoes

SCENE 16

A gravel path. The Queen, The King.

KING: (*At last*) I like this gap
This gap between us
Three feet is it we are apart?
Anyone at a glance can see
THE PROFOUND MISERY THAT CLINGS TO THESE
(*Gravel*)
We have got this right at least
Only two senile bishops engaged upon a fine point of theology could look like us
(*Gravel*)
I'm not senile but let us admit
IT IS THEOLOGY
(*A false laugh from the King. Gravel. He stops suddenly*)
Oh
Oh
(*He snorts, sobs*)

QUEEN: Shh

KING: Yes

QUEEN: Shh

KING: I stopped

QUEEN: Stop if you wish

KING: Yes
Yes
Why not stop
A slave observing us from some pantry window will read my
LET HER READ WHAT SHE WANTS
And my shrunken shoulders
Oh it's all there
Me stooping
You
NEVER STOOPING
Ha
I could
Not could
BUT SHOULD
Quite simply and quite swiftly
THROTTLE YOU NOW MY LOVELY NECK

QUEEN: Yes
KING: Now
Yes
Throttle you and lower you to this dewy ground who could criticize no justice is aesthetics justice is the way things look
(*Pause. A rook*)
QUEEN: You didn't
KING: I didn't
I didn't and it's too late now
Revenge has rhythms
I HAVE NEVER BEEN MORE INFATUATED WITH YOU THAN I AM TODAY BUT YOU MUST DIE
Walk
Walk
(*The gravel*)
QUEEN: Must?
KING: (*Crossly*) MUST MUST OBVIOUSLY
(*He stops*)
Look at you
Look at the belly on you
STOP
(*She stops*)
The perfect rising of it
Lifting like a landscape between the swordblades of your hips
And of course you're
You can't help yourself
POSING TO ADVANTAGE I NEVER KNEW A WOMAN WHO COULD STAND OR WALK LIKE YOU
I've got new shoes for you
(*Rooks*)
QUEEN: *You* have?
KING: I have yes
Oh don't frown
They're Louis Crignon
Listen
A shutter can be slammed on even the most desperate love (*He breathes*)
At the wedding of my daughter and the Prince (*He snorts*)

The Prince of All the Irish I have learned to call (*And again*)
MY SON
You dance for me
For me alone
The whole world watching lords louts all the trays still all the cutlery struck dumb and glasses hanging halfway to their lips

QUEEN: If you wish
KING: I do wish
Your taut arse
Your tense limbs slicing the air in ribbons with each step (*Pause*)
Walk now
Those observing us will think we're quarrelling when we never do
Close the gap now
(*Gravel*)
Close the gap
I SO LOVE YOU BUT YOU HAVE KNOTTED HORRIBLY THE ROPES OF DYNASTY
(*He stops*)
If only you had said some forester did this to you

SCENE 17

A walled garden

SNOW WHITE: This execution
(*Birds*)
This execution's got something to do with shoes
(*Birds*)
So if you see a pair of shoes
WHY DO I TELL YOU THIS
WHY WHEN I HATE YOU
I think you are in love with death I think if you were not in love with it you'd run why don't you run shave your head and be a nun the nuns will shelter you
(*Birds*)

You want to steal my wedding
You stole my father
You stole my husband
And now you want to violate my wedding too
THE CHILD WILL PERISH IF YOU DO
(*Pause*)
Be kind
Run and be kind to me (*Pause*)

QUEEN: Girls run (*Pause*)
SNOW WHITE: You are magnificent and vile and beautiful
and terrible and your corpse will hang over
my entire existence like the shadow of some
long-limbed animal you sprawl there with my
husband's child in you a child you will not
save by running nor yourself by lying let me
love you oh let me love you mother let me
(*Snow White flings herself into the arms of the
queen*)

QUEEN: Death yes
Death I ran towards
Death in every cupboard
Death on every stair
I have met men in cupboards
I have met men on stairs
And this peculiar
UNDRESSING
What is it but a waiting to be killed?
(*A fresh wind*)
The child's my death
Oh don't you see
The single man in all the world whose act
of love could make a pregnancy fatal to me
is your husband-to-be?
Why else did it take so long

SCENE 18

A man weeping incessantly.

QUEEN: Hold the mirror still
OLD WOMAN: It is still lady it's the room that's shaking
(*A wail*)

QUEEN: Yes
                Well does it matter
                (*A wail*)
                I think it does
                I think it does matter
                The dyeing of my hair was less than perfect so
                possibly the styling of it needs to be
                (*A wail*)
                Oh do please weep in the corridor
KING: (*Through a sob*) Darling
                Darling
QUEEN: Yes
JANE: (*Sobs*) I'm sorry
                I'm sorry about the dyeing I was all nerves
QUEEN: Or should it be more casual?
                Perhaps it should be wild?
                As if some storm had battered me?
JANE: I don't know Ma'am
QUEEN: Yes
                Attack it
JANE: Attack it?
QUEEN: Yes
                Attack my hair
                Like this
JANE: Oh Madam
QUEEN: Copy me
JANE: Oh Madam
KING: I'll be all right
                I will be
                (*The old woman cries out*)
                Yes
                Yes
                Odorous old woman we are all so
                Hug me
                Hug me
OLD WOMAN: I'm holding the mirror sir
KING: All right then I'll hug you
                (*A surge of weeping*)

SCENE 19

An empty hall. The heels of the Queen, slow, first in one direction, then another. They cease. The Queen calls

QUEEN:	It's summer isn't it?
	Why have you built a fire like that?
SMITH:	(*Distant*) The windows will be open lady
QUEEN:	(*Walking*) The windows will be open will they
	so why have you built a fire like that?
	Three hundred people will be sitting here
	(*A clang of fire tongs*)
	I'm talking to you
	(*Pause. Her heels*)
SMITH:	Yes
QUEEN:	I'm talking to you and you are looking at the
	floor
SMITH:	I am lady yes
	(*Her heels cease*)
QUEEN:	What ugly hands you have and wrists
	Great wrists
	(*Two paces*)
	Open your lips (*Pause*)
	STILL NOT LOOKING
	And my tongue
	Goes round your teeth
KING:	I'm sorry about the temperature
	(*His footsteps resound on the flagstoned floor*)
	The guests will wilt
	Much unbuttoning I predict
	Varnished bosoms
	Slippery teats
	Snow White even might glow a little pink
	I'm sitting there
	Among the dogs and dwarves
	CAN YOU DO THIS
	CAN YOU DO WHAT YOU MUST DO
	(*The sound of a staff and cries of the officials*)

QUEEN:	(*Horrified*) I must whatever it is you
KING:	Yes
	You are a legend and a legend must
	(*A surge of public noise, rising in volume*)

SCENE 20

The wedding of Snow White and the Prince of all the Irish. A hubbub.

ASKEW:	Take my jacket
JANE:	Sir
ASKEW:	And hang it up don't chuck it
	(*As Jane departs*) Then bring a hanger for my shirt
	I could strip naked
	I could plunge the ornamental lake
YOUNG ASKEW:	WHEREAS I AM CHILLED TO THE BONE
ASKEW:	Yes
YOUNG ASKEW:	Teach me cynicism will you
	What more can a father do for his son
	TEACH ME THE CYNICISM THAT WILL WARM MY LIFE
ASKEW:	You have a bride
	Yesterday you had no bride today you have one that bride is the only mother no other mothers can you make except for girl-grooms chambermaids and snake-hipped waitresses in the shag arcades
	WATCH AND CONQUER HORROR
	PRINCES SQUIRM BUT KINGS MUST WATCH
	(*Pause. Hubbub*)
	In any case
	(*He whispers*)
	You must have felt
	I did
	Trespassing in the Queen's estate
	Travelling her dark fields
	Wading her waters
	We are not alone in here
	I HEARD A GATE (*He half-laughs*)

(*A staff beaten on the stone floor. The hubbub stops*)

KING:
This heat
Irksome as it is
Bewildering to some
Spoiling the pâté
Wilting the salad leaves
(*A mild laugh from the public*)
Is nonetheless
Oh yes
ENTIRELY NECESSARY I ASSURE
YOU
The condition of two ecstasies (*Pause*)
Mine obviously (*Pause*)
But also
Hers (*Pause*)
The Queen will dance
The Queen who walks but rarely dances will
now dance
DANCE YES
And such a
Oh
SUCH A DANCE
As if to show all those who find in her a
synonym for decorum
HER MAD AND UNGOVERNABLE
SELF
Show her the shoes
(*The sound of irons and tongs*)
Oh
They glow
Oh don't they glow
I defy even the most arthritic and recalci-
trant misanthrope to stay still long in these
THEY MAKE YOU LEAP
Is there music?
Did she choose her jig?

QUEEN:
I don't like music (*Pause*)

KING:
No (*Pause*)
No that we had in common
Oh how we laughed to see each other yawn-
ing in the concert hall
WE MUCH PREFERRED

THE SYMPHONY OF THE MARRIAGE
BED
She will dance in silence
Or
In the gasps of our
(*Pause. He is fixed. He recovers*)
Disbelief
The shoes
The shoes must glow
(*The tongs. The fire*)
As for those
The leather heels you are standing in
Amaze us
Let us applaud how standing on the one you
tip the other off with the slight and oh so
familiar jerking of your thumb
(*The Queen walks, stops, tips off a shoe*)
Yes
Yes
(*He leads clapping, spontaneous*)
It's so well done
SHE BALANCES
OH LOVE HER I DO
IRON NOW
IRON SHOE
(*In the silence, the sound of the tongs on iron*)

SMITH:	(*Sotto Voce*) Forgive me lady
	I've no wish to hurt you
QUEEN:	Haven't you?

Can you be sure?
KEEP STILL
You're shaking more than me
KEEP STILL
I CAN'T DO THIS
I CAN'T
I CAN'T
I CAN'T DO THIS
Have you never held a woman's shoe
Just place it on the floor
(*The tongs, the iron heel on stone*)
I lift my hem
I lift my skirt so I can see
(*A terrible cry comes from the King*)

	YELL
	YELL FOR ME
YOUNG ASKEW:	(*In a torrent unleashed by madness*) No conscious being human or animal willingly exposes itself to pain unless this pain is so to speak an instalment against a worse pain still a fox for example trapped in a snare might gnaw through its own
	(*The King emits a worse bellow*)
QUEEN:	Next now
	NEXT
SMITH:	Sorry lady oh sorry
	(*The clang of the iron shoe*)
QUEEN:	STAND IT
	STAND IT ON ITS HEEL
	(*The king bellows*)
SNOW WHITE:	She can
	She can
	She can walk in red hot shoes
	The hatred in my mother oh
YOUNG ASKEW:	(*Pursuing the logic of his argument*) The fox reasons if one can talk of a reasoning fox that however severe the discomfort of the maiming the maiming is when placed in the scales so to speak the scales of competing discomforts less
KING:	NOT DANCING
YOUNG ASKEW:	Less
	I'M NOT LOOKING
	Less
KING:	NOT DANCING IS SHE
YOUNG ASKEW:	Less than the enormity of the prospect of extinction one must conclude therefore that pain is
SNOW WHITE:	It's hatred isn't it hatred makes her able to
KING:	NOT DANCING
	(*A silence but for the heels of the Queen's iron shoes on the stone floor. They ring. They are paced. Her breath is audible. A knife or fork falls. A dog whimpers. The breath continues as the Queen passes out of the great hall. Birds suddenly fill the air with screeching*)

KING: (*Distantly*) NOT DANCING
WAS SHE?

SCENE 21

The terrace. A wind

QUEEN: MIRROR
(*There is no reply*)
MIRROR
(*A wind*)
I did not scream
MIRROR
REFLECT MY PRIDE TO ME

SCENE 22

OLD WOMAN: Coming lady

QUEEN: I'm unforgivable
Even when I am punished I do not weep
SHOW ME THE FACE THAT DOES NOT
WEEP
Injustice has not altered me
As for my feet

OLD WOMAN: Lady it's not your feet

QUEEN: MY FEET ARE HAMS
I'll scream but later
Later on I'll find a place
I'll scream to animals
They won't pretend to pity me
They'll graze
They'll ruminate
I prefer that

OLD WOMAN: LADY YOU ARE BLEEDING UNDER-
NEATH
And I can't stop it
(*Pause. The Queen discovers her miscarriage*)

QUEEN: I am
I am
I thought
How stupid

I thought my pain was in one place
(*The wind*)

SNOW WHITE: Mother
Mother
(*She crouches beside the Queen*)

QUEEN: One must acknowledge your father's perfect cleverness
The beauty of our struggle and my death oh don't think death's a truce
See the bright blood of his cleverness
It shines on you Snow White who is less now less white than me
(*The sound of hounds in a chase*)